AT
FOREST'S
EDGE

AT FOREST'S EDGE

TALES OF HUNTING, FRIENDSHIP, AND THE FUTURE

JOEL SPRING

Skyhorse Publishing

Skyhorse Publishing books may be purchased in bulk at special discounts
for sales promotion, corporate gifts, fund-raising, or educational purposes.
Special editions can also be created to specifications. For details, contact
the Special Sales Department, Skyhorse Publishing, 307 West 36th Street,
11th Floor, New York, NY 10018 or info@skyhorsepublishing.com.

Skyhorse® and Skyhorse Publishing® are registered trademarks of Skyhorse
Publishing, Inc.®, a Delaware corporation.

Visit our website at www.skyhorsepublishing.com.

10 9 8 7 6 5 4 3 2 1

Library of Congress Cataloging-in-Publication Data is available on file.

Cover design by Kai Texel
Cover credit: Michael Ringer

Print ISBN: 978-1-5107-6082-0
Ebook ISBN: 978-1-5107-6749-2

Printed in the United States of America

This book is for my nephew, hunting partner,
and friend, Porter Hunt.
Keep doing what you're doing. The future is bright.

TABLE OF CONTENTS

1

PIER PRESSURE

Old age is like everything else. To make a success of it,
you've got to start young.
—Theodore Roosevelt

I'M GETTING too old for this.

Ahead of me, my younger hunting partners hopped and stepped deftly between ice-covered boulders at the base of the gigantic pier. Of those boulders, there wasn't a single one with a level surface on which to climb. Had it been a dry, warm day, navigating these enormous chunks of rock would have been a challenge. In retrospect, practicing on a warm, dry day would have been a smart move. In reality, the wet, icy boulders were the obstacle course from hell. In between each boulder, the increasingly angry lake sent geysers of icy water up, making the course more interesting. I think the boys found that to be an integral part of the challenge. I'd long ago given up the idea that a face full of icy water—or even falling to my death into that frigid water—was a challenge worth accepting. Since I'd apparently joined a team of duck hunting mountain goats, I had no choice but to plod on. While the boys jumped and laughed, I carefully pulled my ammo box along behind before gingerly placing my old 12-gauge duck gun on the next boulder. Forcing myself slowly forward across the treacherous rock, often on hands and knees, I was soon outdistanced by my hunting partners, who settled into their positions before I was even halfway there. Being the elder statesman in the group, I figured it would probably be unseemly to just sit down and cry, so on I crawled. Water lapped up between the boulders with increasing fury now, so I timed my progress to remain as dry as possible.

At one point a distant voice said, *"Come on, you can do it!"*

Had I been able to identify that voice—which I couldn't because my partners were too far away now—I probably would have responded with a less than statesmanlike reply. *Kids.* Finally reaching the adventurous band of three young duck hunters, I pulled up my gun, trying to compose myself while at the same time attempting to hide my breathlessness. Settling into a most uncomfortable crag between two boulders, I loaded my shotgun and tried to think happy duck hunting thoughts.

I've been a duck hunter for a very long time. Truth be told, though, I hadn't duck hunted the late season in a *very long time.* The Niagara River and Lake Ontario offer some of the best inland diver-duck hunting in the entire world. Bluebills, canvasbacks, scoter, goldeneyes, and old squaw (now referred to by some as the long-tailed duck), as well as several less common species, all visit the area during the late duck season. Mostly fishing and foraging birds, the divers rely upon the only open water in the Northeast to provide hunting grounds when their home areas far to the north are iced over and inaccessible. The area is a major attraction to birds, bird hunters, and birders alike, and I never tire of the endless parade of species visiting our area in the winter. From snowy owls, to harrier hawks, to the extraordinary array of waterfowl, the area just south of Lake Ontario provides a resting spot for many species after a long flight across the big lake. Much less transitory, myself, I've been lucky enough to call the area home for almost my entire life.

Duck hunting in my younger days mostly took place on the shores of Lake Ontario and the banks of the Upper Niagara River. The diversity of ducks on the Niagara during the late-season hunt was incredible. In addition to the plentiful diver ducks and mergansers, mallards often winter over there, providing late-season greenhead shooting that not many northern hunters can enjoy in December and January. Some of my most memorable days were hunting with a group of friends, watching the dogs work the fast, frigid currents, retrieving duck after duck. In retrospect, hunting along the shelf ice was probably as treacherous as today's hunt, especially when someone's dog needed a hoist up and out of the deep, fast-moving water. Even with chest waders, the river often won, spilling over the top of the waders and rendering their insulative factors moot. Slipping off the shelf ice, or tripping when retrieving the decoys at the end of the day, was always challenging with frozen hands. Falling in and taking a cold bath wasn't just a possibility, but a likelihood. I was younger then and, possibly, a lot less smart. But, much like my young hunting partners today, I didn't think much about it. I didn't stop to consider the danger or the consequences. As a result, they were some of the best hunting days of my entire life.

I think that's how it's supposed to work.

With the pre-dawn light growing in the distance, I tried to focus on the surroundings. I forced myself to try not to think about how the hell I was going to get back out of here. When you get older, things like that tend to cross your mind more

often, I've found. The great gray pier stretched out from the
bay into the big lake. Two- and three-foot waves increased in
intensity, lapping against the pier and the boulders, often soaking us in the process. Not good conditions for birding, for certain, this is the kind of day that was made for duck hunting.
The heavy wind would keep the birds moving in the surf and, if
it got any more intense, some of the birds would divert around
the end of the pier and right past our hideout. Ten minutes after
shooting light, a small flock of old squaw passed our decoy
spread. All four guns came up. The guns went down just as
quickly as they banked away. As the speedy diver ducks once
again flickered back in our direction, the guns came up again. I
heard a safety click off.

My nephew Porter, who had organized this trip, was just to
my right. As the click sounded above the crash of the waves,
Porter and I both hissed at the same time, *"Wait!"* When the
ducks cleared half of that distance, we again spoke simultane-
ously, *"Now!"* The flock banked left and the guns roared. Two
drake old squaw fell just outside of the decoys. Another single
bird banked right and I pulled the trigger. It was the first old
squaw I had shot in many years. Three white bellies bobbed in
the surf around the decoys.

After scanning to ensure there were no more incoming for
the moment, Porter scrambled down the rocks and pulled my
large kayak from the place we'd secured it in the rocks before
daylight. Having been berated very recently by his grumpy
Uncle Joel, he dutifully put on his PFD before paddling out
into the relatively calm surf of the channel and retrieving the
trio of divers. Out to his right, a hundred yards into the channel between the two piers, I spotted a dark duck. A quick scan
through the binoculars showed it to be a single mallard drake.
I hollered for Porter, who had almost reached the pier, and
gestured toward the mallard. I just wanted to point it out to

him. As I should have expected, though, he turned the kayak around and paddled directly for the distant bird. By the time he reached it, it was perhaps two hundred yards from shore, bobbing in the increasing waves. Porter's friends and I watched as the bird's comfort zone was finally violated and he took to the wing. The mallard flew at top speed away from the kayak. The duck tumbled, dead. It seemed like a full minute before the concussion of Porter's shot reached us across the water. When he got back, I scrambled (okay, *crawled*) down to meet him, get the ducks, and help him get back out of the kayak. His face was beet-red and the kayak was already covered in a thick coat of ice.

"I didn't think you'd go after it!" I said.

"What did you think I'd do? Let him go?"

I laughed. He laughed. I remember what it was like to be like that. I'm still like that in some ways, but these days, at 52, I'm far less likely to paddle out on to dangerous open water for the slim chance at shooting a single duck. At 24, Porter's age, it would have been a no-brainer. Now, it might take two ducks to get me out there.

The boys and I shot some more divers that morning. I got to tell some old duck hunting stories and they got to tell some newer duck hunting stories. We had a good time, eventually filling the kayak with twenty some-odd ducks, mostly old squaw. I enjoyed watching the interactions of the young hunters. With the excitement and expressiveness of youth, I thought (except for frequently checking their cell phones) that they are not so much different than I was at that age. The thought brought some comfort since the sport of hunting, as we'll talk about later, doesn't always seem to foretell a bright future.

At home that night, I relayed the morning's hunt to Joy, comparing it to my early days of duck hunting with my friend John—who got me into duck and bird hunting in my early 20s.

He was the elder statesman then and, I remarked to Joy, I wondered if that's how he felt when I went along with him and insisted on shooting just one more duck or trying for just one more pheasant before we called it a day.

"But John was only ten years older than you," Joy reminded me. "You are *twice as old* as Porter and his friends."

I thought about that. I don't feel like an old man, but I was certainly the old man in that group during the early morning hours. I don't mind being *the* old man, so much as I'm distressed by the idea of being *an* old man. I tried not to lose any sleep over it. Why? First, there's not much I can do about it. Second, I'm old. I need my rest.

And, I needed to be back out at the pier again at 4 in the morning.

2

AT FOREST'S EDGE

Difficult to see. Always in motion is the future.
—*Yoda*

BACK IN the late eighties and early nineties, you'd be hard pressed to open a hunting magazine and *not* find some reference to hunting the *edges*. The initial writers' intentions were commendable for introducing hunters to the concept of hunting transitional zones for deer. Certainly, deer travel edges. The places those articles' writers described were areas where mature woods interface with secondary growth. They could also be where long grass borders a brushy draw or where heavy bedding cover meets up with a feeding area. Without a doubt, deer trails abound in such areas. But, being a young guy in those days, it was hard not to picture those *edges* as a big stand of woods bordering a wide-open field. I think the mere suggestion of *hunting the edges* conjures up the same vision in many hunters' minds. Though I have no hard scientific data, I

7

think those articles about hunting the edges were responsible for about two million tree stands popping up at the edges of a million different woodlots around the country. It seemed that way, anyway. Of course, the transitional areas can be much less defined than that. Still, when people picture an *edge,* I think they picture a conspicuous edge between two distinctly different types of cover. I do, anyway, so everyone else must see it the same way. Right? Well, maybe not *everyone.*

A lot has been written (some of it by me, in *Strong is the Current*) about the concept of time resembling a river. Relentless in its flow, unstoppable in its forward momentum, time can indeed seem to flow like water. Recently, though, when pondering such philosophical issues, I've begun to think of time somewhat differently. Nature is a continuum of motion, and I think now that time is even more elemental than water. Though I'm sure I'm not the first to come up with such a comparison, I now consider time as a kind of natural trinity: The Past, The Present, and The Future. Of that trinity, The Present is all we can know. Modern and ancient philosophers often declared the past and future are little more than illusions. But, as anyone who has ever lived a little will tell you, the past is full of power. The past may no longer be, but the scars those past days gave us are no less real in the present. What we are in the present is completely shaped by what we've lived in the past. Still, the present is what we must deal with, but we also live in the future. From a mental health perspective, living in the future is a risky proposition. *Hope* for the future can keep us moving along—even helping us survive—while, at the same time *fear* for the future can cause very real bouts of anxiety.

Since we're looking at the future in this book, I've thought long and hard about what it is. It's not an abstract. Just because we may not be here to see it if, say, we choke on a hotdog this afternoon, doesn't make it any less real or less worth contemplating. There's not much we can do to control the future, but it's a foolish person who doesn't at least try to do a little planning.

I've begun to think of the future as a forest.

The present is a golden field. Ahead of me, the dogs endlessly search the long grass for pheasant scent. Moving to the north, though, we happen upon a stand of mature oaks. The oaks are the future. In between us is the gray, thick brush of secondary growth lining the edge of the more mature woods. The thick brush, inaccessible to the marauding combines, still gets enough sunlight that the young growth survives and even thrives. From the field, the forest is dark and impenetrable. That's the future. What is in the forest? Fearful, scary things? Sweet acorns that will feed generations of deer and turkeys? We don't know. We can't know.

The curse of the future, of those hidden woods, is how we can only ever be just on the outside, wondering what lies within. Or, in human terms, what comes next. There's no doubt that one day we'll be in there, dealing with whatever the shadows have to show us but, for now, all we can do is stand at the edge. There's no sense going back. That ground has been covered. But we have not yet moved forward into the unknown. Standing at the edge, we know the future may hold adventure or heartache, triumph or tragedy. But, for today, we just stand in that golden field at forest's edge.

3

SUMMER SOLSTICE

JUNE 21. The longest day of the year.

The summer solstice is upon us. Tomorrow, the days begin to shorten. At first, imperceptibly. For those not tuned in to the rhythms of nature and time, our only hint may have been a quick mention by the local weatherman and subsequently paid little attention. For those living for the excitement of the change in season, more closely attuned to those mystic rhythms, things have already begun to change. The summer's drought brought down many leaves in a parody of the autumn months to come. The daylight will soon be more of a commodity than before the solstice. Those autumn walls will close in, bringing the muted light of fall in the early morning where the sun once shone. Slipping farther and farther away, the sun will migrate south for the winter, settling into the tree line instead of sinking into the big lake at dusk. The wild animals, still in summer coats, will become more active at dawn and dusk now, despite the heat. They know what's coming. The changes are subtle, but present.

Autumn has always been a time of anticipation and preparation for me. Photography season gives way to fishing season which, in turn, gives way to hunting season. The cycle has
repeated itself my whole adult life. I opened the gun safe and
took out some of my old workhorses. The battered old side-
by-side shotgun that has shot birds over every dog I've owned,
and its newer, less battle-scarred replacement, felt good in my
hands, if only for a few moments, as I swung on the imagi-
nary pheasants flying around the back bedroom. The deer rifle
that hadn't seen daylight since last December when it put some
venison in the freezer felt familiar in my hands. It should. The
venison is almost gone now, as it almost always is by the end of
fishing season. The cycle repeats and repeats, an endless outdoor coda.

Before oiling the guns and placing them back into the dark
safe, I picture all of the friends with whom I've shared the
hunting experience. On top of the gun safe are some framed
photos of my old bird dogs. I see their smiling faces, many
years removed, and shed more tears at their absence. They are
the ghosts of autumn. Behind me, watching me closely, are my
golden retriever, Max, and Fred, our springer puppy. Max has
proven himself in the fields for many seasons now, and Fred's
youthful energy will be a helpful addition to Max's aging bones.
Though Fred still lacks in experience, I have no doubt the two
of them will be a great team. Closing my eyes, I can almost see
the golden fields and colorful trees as I walk behind them, trying hard to keep up.

For now, there are more fish to be caught and more creeks
to be paddled. There are more summertime photos to be taken,
with their rich greens and colorful hues. It won't be long, however, before the pale browns, grays, and dry, golden yellows of
fall arrive and, on the heels of that, hunting season.

I'm almost ready.

4

THE NUISANCE HUNT

DEER HUNTING season started early this year. While I don't typically start deer hunting these days until October or November, Porter invited me on a nuisance deer hunt. In July. Deer hunting. In *July.* I'll be the first to admit, I don't generally enjoy warm-weather hunting. I don't relish the thought of sharing the woods with blood-sucking insects when they are at the vampiristic peak. I don't like blackflies in my eyes or mosquitos on my neck. The last few years, as well, we've seen an explosion of the deer tick population. I've never been an avid spring turkey hunter for precisely this reason. Over the years, I've done several early autumn bear hunts, and it was not uncommon to sit in the deep woods waiting for a bear to arrive as temperatures soared up into the 80s and 90s. Because I *love* bear hunting, I was able to tolerate the heat, the blackflies, the no-see-ums, and the mosquitos, but *barely.* I still get the willies envisioning those clouds of blackflies only inches from my face, which was shielded as well as possible by a bug-hood. It was, at times, quite miserable. When Porter asked me to join him, I had my reservations. It had so far been a very warm summer. Almost too warm for fishing, much less hunting. The thought of hunting deer while being sucked dry by swarms of bloodsuckers while waiting for deer to arrive did not appeal to me. The landowner gave Porter a few nuisance permits as a test. If he succeeded in filling a few of them, there would be more permits to come. Porter and I are a pretty good hunting team. We operate on the same wavelength of taking our missions seriously, while still having fun and stopping to admire the trivialities of nature, such as a large fox squirrel, or a bald eagle picking at a deer carcass. We hunt very similarly with the same relentless nature, though being half my age, Porter's relentlessness handily outdistances my own. I can still be relentless, but in an older, slower kind of way. I was honored to be asked along as someone who might be able to fill a permit or two, even if my heart wasn't in it. I did it more for Porter than anything. In the days between the invitation and the hunt, I tried not to picture what it would be like field-dressing deer in the heat of the early evening. I tried not to picture flies on us and the deer as we dragged them across some enormous field. I tried not to picture how hot we'd be by the time that chore was accomplished, if we were successful.

I tried, but it didn't work.

The day before the hunt, Porter and I texted several times. His plan was to scout three big fields. The amount of land held by the landowner was impressive. Thousands of acres, and we would have his sprawling properties all to ourselves. Porter's plan was to shoot only big does that didn't appear to have fawns. I thought that was a good plan, not that I'd put very much thought into the deer management philosophy on this piece of property. *Old does it is,* I thought. Porter is a relentless scouter and, not at all to my surprise, had a few ideas about where we might see the most deer. And by *most deer,* I mean dozens and dozens of deer. The area was crawling with them, and I very well understood the farmer's desire to thin the herd. Vast grain-, corn-, and beanfields stretched for miles. Around most of these fields were dense, creek-bottom bedding areas. The place is a Mecca for deer. Though I'd hunted the general area briefly last year, I hadn't had much of a clue about its vastness. Miles and miles of food were punctuated by hundreds of acres of deer cover. I'd never hunted anywhere quite like it.

After a long stretch of hot, high-humidity days, our late afternoon arrival at the property was met with a cool, northern breeze. It was almost, you might say, *autumnal*. Relieved that we would not, at least, be battling the heat, I felt like things were looking up. I also found myself looking more forward to the hunt. Ahead of us, a large beanfield stretched out almost as far as the eye could see.

"What's the plan?" I asked Porter.

"This field had dozens of deer in it last night. The wind is different tonight, but I think it might still be good. We might be sitting for a while. It's a little early."

Funny, I was thinking that it was a little *late* but what do I know? The golden last hour of light shone against the field and the very distant woodline. Still, I knew that it was perfectly legal to fill the nuisance deer permits until 11 p.m. I had no desire to shoot with a spotlight but, if that was our only option, I would play along. To me, that was a little too similar to everything I know about *poaching*. But, if it was legal and that's what it took to fill Porter's tags, I supposed I would lower my sporting standards a bit, just for this special occasion.

As if reading my mind, Porter said, "This really is like legalized poaching."

"Well," I replied, "let's see what happens. Maybe we'll fill our permits before dark."

He nodded and again reminded me, "Big, dry does, right?"

I nodded in return. *Okay with me.*

Settling into the long grass bordering the field, we didn't have to wait long and, thankfully, it didn't appear as if we'd need that spotlight after all. A lone doe appeared at one of the near corners of the field. Perhaps five hundred yards out, she glowed orange in the waning rays of daylight. Porter, whose scope is quite a bit more powerful than my own, said, "She's big. No fawns." We debated what to do. Putting the sneak on her now, we may well spook other deer off before they got out into the field. It was a dilemma, but she was certainly the kind of deer we wanted to shoot. *What to do, what to do?* Porter looked conflicted. A deer in the hand is worth a few dozen in the brush but, still, he had hoped to fill multiple permits that evening.

I pointed out the large, mostly dry, irrigation ditch spanning the length of the field almost directly from us to the big doe. "We could sneak down that ditch and try to get within range. As long as we stay low, we shouldn't spook anything else coming out into the field." On cue, two more adult does joined the one in the field. Two fawns trailed closely behind. Now, it would be five pairs of eyes to evade but if we were stealthy, I thought, we could probably get within range. Porter is excellent at long shots. I don't practice them enough to be good at long shots and prefer to bring it inside two hundred yards if at all possible. We whispered back and forth on that topic. Porter wanted me to shoot first, since he'd already filled a couple of nuisance tags. I told him I didn't care who shot first, but he insisted. He said he only wanted to shoot if I had already dropped one. How often do things work out that perfectly? For me, it's a rarity, but I agreed anyway.

Deer hunting in July, I thought again. *Who would have thought?*

Starting the sneak down the deep ditch, we kept low. Porter

was crouched impossibly far down, like a tiger. I was bent awkwardly at the waist, like a 52-year-old man with a bad back. Without discussion, Porter stayed in the lead, popping carefully up now and then to see how we were progressing and to ensure that the deer were still there. The cool north breeze blew directly into our faces, perfect for the stalk. We covered a hundred yards or more, when Porter again stood and motioned me to do the same. Deer streamed into the field across from us and behind us, from two different directions. A quick glance downfield revealed the five deer we'd been monitoring had moved slightly off now, feeding slowly away from the ditch. To make matters worse, the lone doe who was our initial objective had mixed in with the other two does and fawns. Though she stood slightly higher than the other two adults, it was difficult to differentiate between them. Neither of us wanted to shoot a doe with a fawn.

Risking giving away our location, we scrambled up the side of the ditch and hid in the long grass near the edge of the beanfield.

"The one all the way to the left is our deer," Porter said.

"How far?" I asked.

"Still probably two-fifty."

"I'd like to pull in closer before taking the shot."

If Porter was impatient with me, he was polite about it. I think he'd rather be hunting with someone wanting to *make* a good shot, rather than with someone who was willing to *try*. We whispered and strategized a bit more. While we did that, the five deer in our sights trotted off another hundred yards in the wrong direction.

"Go ahead and take it," I said, knowing he could easily make the shot.

"No. There's a lot of deer in the field. We have time."

I didn't argue with him. The field held well over twenty deer now, with more deer emerging from the brush on three of the four sides. He pointed out two very large does trotting in from the far side, perhaps four hundred yards distant. Unlike the other deer, they did not pause to eat once inside the field. For whatever reason (to this day, I do not know), they continued at a brisk pace across the field, quartering across in front of us. What little breeze remaining died off and, even at a distance, we could clearly hear their legs crashing through the beans. They suddenly turned directly toward us.

"Here they come!" Porter whispered.

"Shooters?"

"Both of them," he said. He may have been breathing heavily. Or maybe that was me.

As the first of the two big does got within one hundred yards, trotting directly at us, I said, "I'm going to take the first one."

"Wait a second, if you can," Porter replied, surprising me. "Maybe we can get them both."

My safety was already off, and I left it that way. The doe's neck was perfectly aligned in the crosshairs. The distance dropped from ninety yards, to fifty, then twenty. This was not a slow-motion dream sequence. Rather, it was unfolding impossibly quickly. The doe loomed so large in my scope, I had no choice but to either shoot or let her overrun our hiding spot and, ultimately, get away. I shot quickly and the lead doe cartwheeled into the beanfield. Only a handful of seconds passed, and Porter's rifle roared in my right ear. The second doe slid to a stop just yards from the first. It was a perfect double. I'm not a big high-fiver, but Porter and I high-fived. We might even have given each other unsightly man-hugs. I don't remember . . .

There would be buggy, sweaty field-dressing and quartering to do in the glow of the headlights of Porter's truck. For right now, though, in the encroaching darkness with the two big does at my feet and my young hunting partner admiring them and checking their teeth for age, I felt a surprising sense of satisfaction. What hadn't been an eagerly anticipated hunt turned into an evening of unpredictable stalking, adventure, and surprise.

It was much more of a *deer hunt* than I ever expected.

5

GAMBLING ON THE RAIN

It HAD rained so many days in a row, I almost didn't recognize the sun.

Gambling on the weather is an inextricable part of scheduling vacation time around hunting season. It seems like such a good idea at the time. In January, my co-workers and I begin deciding who will take what time and when. My July Adirondack vacation is a given. I also try very hard every year to get opening week of pheasant season and opening week of deer season. Any leftover vacation days are generally split between fishing and hunting. When enjoying the warmth of summer, I look at those hunting weeks on the calendar longingly, wishing they would come more quickly. Every now and then, I realize I am wishing the days away and come to the realization that the best weather of the year is when I spend my waking hours looking forward to some of the *worst* days of the year. One of these years, I'm going to learn to embrace living in the moment. I'm not there yet.

I always tell my hunting partners that some of the best pheasant hunting I've ever had has been in the rain. It's not untrue.

Rather, it's more a function of the fact that in late October and early November, there is typically at least one period of cold, nasty rain. And, since I've spent my valuable vacation time to bird hunt, I don't let that cold, nasty rain stop me. I could throw a dart at the calendar, pick a random day to hunt in that time period, and could almost guarantee a nice, soaking rain. Or, more likely, a *not very nice* rainy day, likely accompanied by a stiff northern breeze. I bird hunt a lot in the rain, so it's no mistake that some of my best days have been in the rain. I try to ignore the fact that some of my *worst* days have also been in the rain. But who wants to count *bad* days? Not me.

Opening Saturday had been a beautiful, cool day. When looking forward to pheasant season, these are the days I see in my mind's eye. A pleasant, sunny Saturday under deep, autumnal blue skies, put two birds in our vests and made for two very happy pheasant dogs. It was the last time Joy got out with me. In the interim, we had a cold, windy Monday, a rainy Tuesday and Wednesday, a dismal rain-snow mix driven by wind on Thursday. Friday again showed good weather, but we couldn't hunt.

A week later, Joy joined me again in the field. It was as if all I needed to do was have her along with me in order that I might get a little good weather. From her perspective, I'm sure, this pheasant hunting thing isn't all that difficult. She went from one sunny, cool and dry hunt to the next. Though I'm sure she was aware, by way of my complaining and all of the soaking wet clothes hung around the fire to dry every night, I may have a slightly different take on the state of Pheasant Hunting 2019.

The dogs coursed enthusiastically ahead of us in the long grass, pausing here and there at a patch of brush to ferret out any hidden birds. While Fred and Max are nowhere near as soured by inclement weather as their human companions, they also seemed to enjoy the reprieve from the rain. The first rooster flushed only a half-hour into our walk. Max retrieved it in his usual graceful style. There was, however, no time for photos as Fred was already back on scent. Since we were still close to the first flush, I thought he might be on old scent from that bird. I was proven wrong when the bird went out between Joy and me, headed for a small woodlot. By the time we were on it, it was a bit of a poke, but the bird crumpled and went down. Fred was on it instantly. I don't think Max liked that. Growling and snarling erupted out of sight in the long grass near the bird. Joy and I both yelled for the dogs, who retrieved the bird together, Fred by the head, and Max by the tail. They were both growling. It wasn't pretty, but I credited them each with a half-retrieve. I didn't yell at either of them for their bad manners until I took the bird, kneeling, and they both tackled me to the ground as I was putting it in my vest. Off balance with my arm reached around my back and into the vest, I went down like a ton of bricks. It's hard to be mad at dogs who are working so hard for you, so I tried to keep the positive reinforcement going as I picked myself up off the ground. At least the ground was dry this time.

"Good boys. Go get some more."

The dogs circled the same spot and I wondered if we were about to get a third. Eventually, though, they picked up on another scent trail that went down an old irrigation ditch and into an adjacent field. The sun shone on the brown oak leaves along the ditch. Farther out, along the creek, the golden field was bordered on the far side by yellow poplars, glowing in the morning light. Joy, more a fan of watching the dogs work than shooting pheasants I suspect, watched the dogs vaulting through the long grass. Fred took to the air several times in his impossible high jumps to check back on us. Joy's smile was wide, radiant. I watched her watching the dogs, with the backdrop of autumn all around us, and took a moment just to breathe it all in. Rainy days might come more frequently, but it is days like these, moments like these, seconds like these, that live in my head rent-free all year round. When the third bird went up, and then went down, I was completely lost in the moment.

I barely remember shooting.

6

OVERBOOKED

I'VE HUNTED alone a lot. For that matter, I generally fish alone more than I fish with others. Being alone with my thoughts tends to lend itself well to the type of writing I do. Much like when I sit down to tinker on a piano or pluck out chords on my guitar, I tend to write in minor keys. Most of my writing about hunting has been in melancholy tones, about the changes of the season, the loss of dogs and old friends and the way life tends to whiz mercilessly by, at times threatening to leave us behind. If you're a reader of my writing, you might picture this introverted guy, sitting alone out in the woods lost in thought while pondering the deeper realities of existence.

Um . . . no.

I'm sure that the people who hunt with me read my books and wonder where all these thoughts come from, if they think about it at all. The guy they know swears like a drunken sailor after a certain amount of bad luck, and is often quite silly. Like most non-fiction writers, I write myself a lot better than I actually am. It's my book, I figure, so I can portray myself as I want to be. It's the selfish side of owning a literary license. If someone else were to write a book and talk about me, I'm certain that book would be altogether different. Though I like being alone, I'm not an introvert. While I like being one with my thoughts, I do most of my deep thinking on insomnia-wracked nights, not while out in the woods or in the pheasant fields. I like being with people. Specifically, I like hunting and fishing with others. I like the camaraderie. I like having someone else to share the fields with so I'm not the only one missing easy shots at birds. I like deer hunting with others for the same reasons. The presence of a partner ensures I'll have help dragging a deer out of the more remote places I hunt.

With the death of my daughter in 2016, I made a point to reach out even more often to my hunting and fishing friends. It's easier to not get bogged down in your own thoughts when a friend is along to cheer you up. At the very least, they can distract you from those ugly thoughts, and back into more mundane chit-chat. While I only deer hunt with a select handful of people, I make it a point to have open invitations when it comes to bird hunting.

In my home area, the pheasant hunting can be meager. There are pockets of wild birds, but a lot of our present-day bird hunting takes place on state land where birds are managed and often stocked. Western New York used to have a rich tradition of pheasant hunting and a huge flock of wild birds. Kids used to take opening day of pheasant season off from school to hunt with their parents and family. Due to the influx of coyotes and the agriculturally affected loss of nesting habitat, that tradition and the culture of pheasant hunting in our area have faded into an artifact of the past, sadly. We do well every year, with the dogs flushing upwards of thirty birds during our very short season. A successful year sees usually between fifteen and thirty birds taken between my hunting partners and myself. By

Midwest standards, that is not great hunting. By Western New York standards, however, it *is*. Because of the limited opportunities to hunt pheasants, it's simply not on most hunters' radar these days. Every time I invite someone new to pheasant hunt the answer is some variation of, "Pheasants? There are pheasants around here?"

In the last few years, I've turned a few friends into bird hunters, even if they had to be dragged kicking and screaming. I feel especially good about a couple of them who have younger kids—some of hunting age, some not quite yet there—and I believe I'm doing my part to pass on the remnants of this tradition. A few of my other die-hard hunting friends will also join me a couple of times a year. I suspect a couple of them may just be humoring *me* rather than exhibiting any insatiable desire to follow Max and Fred around some wet, muddy field. If that's the case, though, they do Oscar-worthy jobs of pretending they're having a good time.

For some reason I still don't quite understand, New York State opted to start most hunting seasons on Saturday the last few years, instead of the traditional Monday opener. I know that hunter numbers are rapidly dropping off and I get that the state is trying to encourage hunters who might want to hunt, but not enough to take a day off. Still, I miss the traditional Monday start to bird (and deer) season. It always seemed like the Monday openers saw the more dedicated hunters in the field. The hunters that planned their vacation time around hunting season. The *serious* hunters. I'm not a hunting snob, but the Saturday opener definitely has a few guys out in the field that simply thought, "Sure, I'm not doing anything Saturday. Let's go." I agree with the state that we need to get more people out there and involved in the outdoor sports but, at the same time, I tend to be (at least internally) a little protective of my hunting areas and hate to see them overrun by weekend warriors. I've

tried to keep my own traditions alive by taking (as I did back in
the Monday opener days) the entire first week of pheasant season and deer gun season off. Although I hunt those busy, often
crowded (especially on state land) opening weekends, Monday
morning I treat as Opening Day Number Two. It scratches
the itch for the traditional hunt, if only in my own intellectu-
ally challenged mind. Often, because of the readily accessible
Saturday opener, there are very few hunters in the pheasant
fields on Monday. *Perfect.*

Opening weekend, I spend my time hunting with Joy. She
enjoys watching the dogs work, and we do well on those as-yet
unpressured birds. Usually on Sunday night, I'll send out texts
to my other hunting friends inviting them to hunt. I tend to keep
Monday to myself, but I offer anyone who wants to go out to
join me Tuesday, Wednesday, and Thursday. I don't try too hard
to juggle one friend or the other. If three of us end up out in
the field, I'm fine with that. Even four guns are not too many.
Fred and Max can easily cover four people. And, with three or
four guns, the likelihood of connecting on a flushed bird is sub-
stantially higher than if it was just me alone with my meager
shooting skills. Fred and Max aren't fazed by more people in
the field. They just want to hunt. People are often too busy to
join me, so the number typically stays just right.

Well, almost always.

In 2018, I sent individual texts out to multiple friends giving
them the typical invitation for a Tuesday afternoon hunt: "Want
to bird hunt Tuesday afternoon?" In addition to bird hunting, I'd
also stumbled onto some highly active, autumn-feeding monster pike in a local Lake Ontario harbor. Needing to get some
photos for a fishing seminar I was giving that winter, I couldn't
resist the opportunity to target those huge, aggressive pike. I'd
pike fish the morning and pheasant hunt the afternoon. It was a
solid plan that reminded me just how much I would love to be

able to retire early. When the replies started rolling in for the afternoon hunt invitation, I was more than surprised. *Everyone said yes.* Dave replied that he wanted to come but asked if he could bring his son Joe. He wanted to try to get him his first pheasant. *Yes!* Keith replied, but said he'd have his young son Barrett in tow and asked if that was okay. Barrett sat in on a duck hunt with us and on that windy, rainy, duck-less day, was a perfectly behaved kid. *Of course!* Then my writer friend, Bill, texted that he'd meet us at the field. *See you there!*

Everyone said yes. And I said yes to everyone.

Well, that's a first.

I talked it over with Max and Fred. They did not mind the prospect of hunting over six hunters and five guns. In fact, they were quite okay with it, evidenced by the way their ears perked up each time the word *bird* popped up during the discussion. I could have broken the hunt down into morning and afternoon but, with the temperatures promising to be in the upper 60s and low 70s, I knew the dogs couldn't tolerate a full day of hunting over multiple guns. And, more selfishly, I didn't want to give up the opportunity to get the kayak out on the open water and take full advantage of the warm weather and, especially, those big pike.

I told the dogs to rest up.

Meeting at the field just after noon, it was already north of 70°F. Hunting jackets were traded for t-shirts and re-introductions were made as we realized this was the same combination of hunters (minus Joe) that got together for the windy-day duck hunt the previous year. Hunting with six people in some big, Midwestern field is not a logistical feat. In the tighter cover and smaller fields of our area, however, we soon found it to be a bit more crowded than even I expected. Early on, Max flushed a big, beautiful rooster. It was within range for a moment, but no one swung on it. I had hung back, hoping for the other guys to get a shot. My trigger finger twitched involuntarily. Pheasant hunting on a 40°F. day, it's easy to work up a sweat following two eager bird dogs. On a 70°F. day with an hour of walking under our belts, everyone was sweating, frequently taking their hats off to fan sweaty, red faces. I don't like to run the dogs above 65°F. but, with frequent water stops, they seemed none the worse for wear. They may even have enjoyed it.

In another hour, the group dissolved from a neat line of hunters to a few small groups wandering around a field. Dave and Joe paused frequently to film the dogs working with their phones. Keith plodded along with Barrett a few steps behind him. Barrett paused frequently to check his phone in the shade of his father's shadow. Bill and I walked along, talking about writing and fishing. Truth be told, other than Max and Fred, we were all a little bored. It happens. Still, it was good to be out there on a multi-generational hunt, talking with my old friends and their offspring. It's the kind of camaraderie I miss on those lonely days that tend to end up in my writing more often.

When the second bird went up a hundred yards out, no one had been watching the dogs. My cardinal rule of *pay attention to the dogs* had gone out the window. Max looked back at me in exasperation as Fred raced off after the rapidly departing rooster. I held my hands up to signal Max. *Sorry, pal.* When he stopped back for a sip of water out of the bottle in my hunting vest, his tail was still wagging. It took a while before Fred returned to us but, with that youthful springer energy, it was probably good for him to work his frustrations out chasing down that wild bird.

Bill had to depart early and, once he left, the group swung back toward the truck, agreeing that it was too warm to continue. The small group changed configurations here and there. I hung back and took some photos, then joined Dave and Joe. Dave and I talked cameras. Then Keith and Barrett worked their way toward me and Keith and I talked about work, which is also against my pheasant-hunting rules and especially when I'm on vacation, but I made an exception because it was anything but a typical day. Back at the trucks, the other hunters lavished attention on Fred and Max before everyone got into their respective vehicles and disappeared back into their normal lives.

For a few moments, I sat on the tailgate of the truck as I have a thousand times at this spot, and let the slight, cool breeze off Lake Ontario refresh me as the dogs panted at my feet, drinking copious amounts of water. As I often do at this sacred place, I closed my eyes and thought about the old friends and long-gone dogs that have traversed these very fields with me. The ghosts of autumn walk freely here. Pivoting back into the present, I patted the dogs, thanking them for their underappreciated hard work in flushing two un-shot birds under less-than-ideal conditions. I promised them the next day, I *would* shoot them a couple of birds. It's a promise that I may well have not been able to keep, since I'd be once again hunting alone the next two days, but they seemed happy enough about the possibility. Hunting dogs are easily motivated. Moving from the past, through the present, I thought briefly about the future, which I do a lot these days. I thought of Joe, already enjoying the hunting sports, and Barrett, dutifully tagging along with his hunter-dad and being a good sport about it.

In this uncertain world, there is hope.

7

TUESDAY'S BIRDS

Solitude is painful when one is young, but delightful when one is more mature.
—Albert Einstein

IN PREPARATION for this book, I spent a few hours reading the first book I wrote that was focused solely on bird hunting, *Thursday's Bird.* While that book tells a few stories of hunting birds with the small circle of friends I had in 2000 and 2001, it was remarkable to me in re-reading just how often I hunted alone. Solitude and meditation always struck the right keys with me back then. They still do. It's a gift to spend time alone in the lonely landscape. It's also a gift to be able to spend time alone with your own thoughts and even more a treasure to take the time to process those thoughts and get some small glimpse at what you're all about. *Finding yourself,* the New Age crowd might say. I found myself some time ago, and I attribute that mostly to my time spent alone or in the pleasant company of dogs. It is as close to being alone yet being with friends that you will ever discover.

I mentioned earlier in the book that, since Jen's death, I try to fill my hunting days with friendship. It's worked and, I will admit, I have more hunting friends than I thought. At times, it seemed forced to ask others to join me since my default is being alone. Still, it's good some days *not* to spend time alone with anger, bitterness, and self-destructive thoughts. Sometimes it's good to be part of a team, whether you like it or not.

As the years since Jen's loss grind on, however, I'm beginning to discover the joy of solitude once again. I used to embrace it. Then I became fearful of it. Now, I'm welcoming solitude back into my life as if it was, itself, a long-lost friend. There is joy in solitude. I think, as a society, we've become deathly averse to removing ourselves even for a short while. Social media has not helped. But, as I'm again realizing, solitude is what every human heart needs to reset itself. To readjust and recalibrate. In the end, we'll never be healthy if we can't stand to be alone with ourselves and our thoughts.

Heading into the familiar long grass of the familiar fields of the familiar public hunting area with familiar hopeful thoughts on my mind, my mental health restored to something, well . . . familiar. In short, it was just good to be here. When I take friends or family, or family and friends, I tend to take a familiar route. A few years ago, I tracked it on my GPS to the tune of five and a half miles. That takes into account working several big fields, a few small thickets, and a long path along the edge of a Lake Ontario tributary. Anything but a creature of habit, I'd nonetheless made that *exact* route dozens of times. When I'm hunting with guests, it's the surest bet to make certain they get a shot at a pheasant or two. Hunting alone is a different story. I start from the beginning of that route, but only stick to it to the extent that the dogs find scent there. When I hunt alone, I zig and I zag. Very often, I backtrack. I don't try to make sense of anything, other than going where Fred and (especially) Max say we should go. If we walk through the same briar patch ten times because the dogs have suggested we do so, we walk ten times through the same briar patch. If I had other hunters with me, they'd likely think to themselves *what the hell are we doing* after the third pass through the same unproductive cover. When it's just the dogs and me? I go wherever they suggest we go. And, usually, we get more birds. After another stretch of rainy, cold days, it was a rare treat to enjoy a frosty, cold morning. While the underbrush wasn't dry, it was at least passably frozen. After drying clothes on the basement line day after day after day, it would be great to go home in clothes that didn't have twenty extra pounds in water weight.

Fred was the first on bird scent. Still learning, and not fully confident in his own abilities, he crossed scent twice on a deer trail between two red-osier dogwood stands. I watched him carefully, more confident in his nose than he was. Fred grunted and snorted, his short stubby tail wiggling like he was getting paid by the wag. Max, too, paused, watching Fred work the ground scent. Max didn't pause for very long before bursting into the cover Fred was working. A couple of quick sniffs, and Max was on the scent. Unlike the younger dog, Max was decisive, instantly picking up the direction the bird had gone. I watched him closely. Fred was still ten yards behind when Max suddenly started snorting. If I'd been hunting with others, I would have said *get ready!* But it was just me, so I got ready. Max dashed left and right, showing none of his nine years as he tore the fresh bird scent apart. Like a bulldozer, he dove into another small patch of dogwood. I pulled my right glove off with my teeth and it fell to the snowy earth by my feet. When the rooster went up, I heard it first. There was cackling and thunderous wingbeats. It took a moment for the bird to clear the four-foot-high brush before I saw it, long enough that I thought Max might catch it before it took to the air. He didn't. Dodging between two maple trees, the bird gave me a poor shot. Heading away, already at top speed, there wasn't much of a window. My side-by-side snapped up, the safety was thumbed forward, and my brain—now fully engaged—somehow calculated the crossing-away lead and dropped the bird at almost forty yards. I've missed much easier shots. *Much* easier shots. In a puff of feathers, the rooster pheasant went down. I looked around, wishing only for a very fleeting moment someone had been there to see the shot. The cover was thick, and it took Max a moment to find the bird. I didn't point, didn't guide. I didn't do any of the stuff you might see in a dog-training book. Max found the bird and brought it back through the thicket. There were a few low growls as Fred nipped alternately at the bird and Max's shoulders, but the retrieve was pulled off splendidly, with a fair amount of decorum. Once Max dropped it at my feet, Fred picked it up and ran a circle around me and *also* dropped it at my feet. I didn't mind. At least he had the idea he should bring me a bird. They both got their share of *good boys*. I think Max knew that they were mostly directed at him. To be fair, Max conceded, Fred *did* find the bird scent. I love hunting with my dogs and my heart swelled with a bit of pride at the sight of my dogs clicking as a bird hunting team.

There was a little less beauty and a little less decorum upon finding the next bird. While Max and Fred sifted the brush to my left, a dark shadow in the snow-dusted ground to the right caught my eye. Thirty yards out, a silhouette was slightly out of place in the shadow of a small dogwood bush. *Rabbit?* No. *Pheasant.* It didn't look big, so I wondered if it was a hen pheasant, not legal to shoot in this area. Then, I realized it was in about four inches of snow, which made it seem smaller than it was. As my eyes adjusted to the shadows, I realized it was a big rooster pheasant. I froze, not wanting to spook the bird, and hoping that Max and Fred would eventually work their way over to it. They were, unfortunately, working other scent. I waited impatiently, wanting to give them the benefit of the doubt if it turned out they were also working on another bird. When they grew bored with their scent trail, the dogs both checked back with me. With a stern hand gesture toward the cover to my right, Fred and Max bounded in. I watched the bird start sneaking away before they found the scent. When they *did* find the rooster's trail, they were on him in seconds. His cackle pierced the cold, quiet air. Towering above the frosty brush in the cold, orange morning light, the rooster crumpled as I touched the trigger. It was the kind of scene that pheasant hunting memories are made of. We'd only been there less than an hour and our two-bird limit was complete. The bird, shot just above both dogs' heads, fell into their waiting jaws. Max had it by the body, and Fred had it by the tail and, together, that's how they retrieved it. It took a moment to convince either of them to let go.

I sat on the ground, carefully prying the bird out of the two eager dogs' jaws as they half-heartedly growled at each other. Maybe they were growling at me. It's possible. After a short photo session, we sat quietly in the snow for a few moments. The day's hunt was over early. Fred and Max jumped enthusiastically at my vest, sniffing at the two big birds hidden within. As Max hit the back of my legs and nearly knocked me to the ground, Fred mugged me in an excited frontal assault. I guess it would be silly to say that I was glad to have this morning *alone*.

8

THE OUTDOOR WRITER

It is useful to go out in this world and see it from the
perspective of another . . .
—Terry Pratchett

I HAVE always disliked the term *outdoor writer*. On the surface, it conjures an image of some poor soul sitting on a rock, pounding away at his old manual typewriter while a bird perches on his head and deer frolic in a nearby meadow. Seriously, though, why can't writers just be writers? Stephen King is forever known as *Horror Novelist Stephen King*. It doesn't matter that he's written drama, science fiction, and one of my all-time favorite books on the subject *of* writing. I mean, he's worth millions and I doubt he sweats the title he's been given too much but deep down I bet he just wishes he was known as a *writer*. I'm several dozen books behind King in output, but the term outdoor writer occasionally gives me heartburn. I'm not really sure why. Maybe it's because I've written other stuff. I've written a

39

lot of technical manuals. I recently wrote an e-book on wildlife
photography. Once, I even wrote a novel which, although it
wasn't intended as horror, was judged by my friends and family
to be quite *horrible*. Still, at this late date, I suppose I'll always
be an outdoor writer whether I like it or not. Last year, I threw
my hands up just a bit further in surrender and joined the New
York State Outdoor Writer's Association, after years of politely
declining the urgings of a friend. Recently, I gave a seminar at
a fishing expo in Niagara Falls, New York. On the promotional
material, it was *Joel Spring, Outdoor Writer*. Most of my writing is about hunting and fishing, mostly because those are the
things about which I'm passionate and most inspired to write.
Usually. Not always. So, I guess that's what I am. I'm an outdoor writer. Argh.

I take my writing life seriously for most of the year but concentrate my efforts on writing most intensively in January,
February, and March. They're the few months between, when
there isn't much left to hunt and not much yet for which to fish.
It's good timing. Winters are for writing and wildlife photography. Besides, since my most recent books are all non-fiction,
the hunting and fishing seasons are when I build up notebooks
and materials for what I hope will be my next book. I take
notes about most of my outings and try to think of a theme in
which I can fold all of that material and make it something that
a stranger might want to read. I thought about this book for six
months before I began tapping away on the keys. In the active
months, I generated a few magazine articles, but I also spent
a lot of time turning over this idea of hunting, the future, and
aging. Just a few weeks before sitting down to begin work on
the first of the year, I had a pretty good idea of what I wanted
to say.

The writing technique for my last four books has been about
the same. I set myself a one-thousand-word daily goal and try

to write every day. I type fast, and I write fast, so it's pretty easy to hit that goal in about an hour. I often double that number if I'm really inspired and cranking. I've had writer friends (*outdoor writers,* as well as *real* writers) who don't find writing enjoyable. I can't imagine spending so much time doing something that's not enjoyable. I love to write. To paraphrase another writer, I write to see what I think. Writing exists on a different plane than thinking. Sometimes I have no idea where the good stuff (and often, the bad stuff) comes from, but it's fascinating to read it after the fact. Oh, are you not supposed to read your own writing? Well, I do. I always cast a suspicious eye toward writers who say they don't go back and read their own writing. It's like all those too-cool movie stars who claim not to watch their own films. *Yeah, right, buddy.* How can you learn to be better unless you go back and take a look at your failures, as well as your successes?

The only way in which writing is *work* for me instead of pleasure is in the preparation. Sometime before getting to work on a book, I make a list of potential chapters from my hunting and fishing notes until I reach a number that's somewhere in the neighborhood of a book in length. Each day, I try to hit my one-thousand-word goal. Once that's done, I use a technique called *clustering* (I know—it makes me laugh, too!) to make specific notes for the next day's writing. Each day, I work my job, do my normal household and dog-related duties, but I'm also weighed down with a giant thought bubble hanging over my head. My brain is full and working overtime to try to figure out *how* I want to say *what* I want to say. I might only write for an hour or two, but I've been thinking about what I'm going to write all day. It can be a heavy burden. I know my friends and family probably notice the difference when I'm in writing mode. I'm not very attentive. Sometimes it's like people are speaking to me from the far side of that distant ravine where I deer hunt so often. And sometimes I don't hear them at all. I try hard to be my normal self, but when I'm my writing self, it wouldn't be accurate to say that I am successful in that endeavor.

Writers are typically weird and *outdoor* writers are not immune.

Over the years, I've written about my outings with all of my hunting partners at one time or another. My old friend John has appeared in more magazine articles and books than any other single person I can name. He's always a good sport about it. Only a few times over the years has one of my friends read a chapter in a book or a magazine article and said, "Wait a second . . . that's not how it happened." One friend in particular seemed to have a mind like a steel trap and would point out my inconsistencies each and every time he found one. It happened so frequently that I started using the line, *then write your own damned story,* on him. It didn't stop him. Remembering things in different ways is all part of the human condition, not just the writing condition. Well-known in the crime field, the Rashomon Effect. That is to say, eyewitnesses are usually unreliable, with four witnesses each describing an event four different ways. On top of our very human unreliability, events are remembered through our own set of filters, and against our own backdrop of emotion. I did some informal research on this a few days ago, and it turns out that much of our memory is based on our frame of mind while experiencing the same things. The more emotionally attached you are to an activity (like bird hunting over my dogs in a place I consider sacred), the more likely you are to experience that activity in a different way. I've seen it called both *selective perception* and *subjective perception.* One of my guest hunters may just be walking along having fun and thinking about dinner, while I'm having a deep emotional moment, or vice versa. It happens. Without a doubt, we would each remember the day differently.

Until recently, I didn't have any writing friends who hunted with me on a regular basis. Now I do. Enter my friend, Bill. Bill is a local outdoor (there's that word again!) columnist with a lifelong reputation in our area. Although we'd spoken in the past when I had new book releases, our friendship really only kindled after he joined me on a pheasant hunt a few years ago. We hit it off, and have since hunted many times together, both for birds and deer. But that first day, a blisteringly warm, unsuccessful hunt over Max (Fred wasn't yet in the picture), I knew right away it would be the start of a good friendship. Bill is quiet. He's thoughtful. He is one of those people who listens to you speak and replies, rather than just waiting for an opening to blurt out his own opinion on the subject, as so many people are fond of doing these days. He never strikes me as a person with an agenda. But, of course, he has one.

He's an outdoor writer.

That first afternoon, after our too-warm pheasant hunt, Max drank deeply from his water bowl at the tailgate of my truck. Bill looked around the golden fields, punctuated by browning oak leaves in the big hedgerows.

"Do you mind if I write about this?" he asked.

"Of course not."

I thought for a moment (not wanting to be a blurter), and stopped myself from adding, *I never ask my friends!* It has never dawned on me to ask if people mind being written about. I think most of my hunting friends just *assume* they're going to be written about if they invite me along, or if they come along on one of my excursions. Maybe I should start asking. The following week, Bill wrote a heartfelt column in the *Buffalo News*. I didn't realize it was there until I started getting texts from several other friends about Max being famous. I walked across the street from my office and bought the paper. There, in the *outdoors* section, was a large photo of Max grinning in the golden grass. I eagerly read the accompanying story, smiling at the details. It's always fascinating to know what someone was thinking during a shared event. Writers are good for that. Bill's memory of the event was slightly different than my own, but it was just seen through his own filter. Nothing was incorrect about it. It just took a different slant than my own memories. That did not surprise me.

Since that day, Bill has stopped asking my permission and has often written about our bird and deer hunts in the local paper. It's nice to see events from someone else's perspective once in a while, and it's notable how different those perspectives can be. As for the friend who used to correct my version of events all the time? He stopped hunting with me several years ago. I don't blame him.

Writers are weird.

9

THE SPLIT

Success consists of going from failure to failure
without loss of enthusiasm.
—Winston Churchhill

I WAS beginning to get a complex.

With two hunts under our collective belts, I had not been able to put my writer-friend Bill on a bird. Knowing now that our hunting exploits were likely to be retold in Bill's newspaper column, I was beginning to feel the heat. The heat was, in fact, part of the problem. An unseasonably warm stretch of October made the dogs tire easily, and hunt a bit less enthusiastically than they do with a chill in the air and frozen ground under their feet. There also seemed to be fewer birds available. In this same spot on my solo hunts, however, I had managed to put one or two in the vest each day. I stopped reporting my successes to Bill, when he twice replied, *are you saving any for me?* After one of those two-bird days, when I'd seen a few other roosters on the way out, I thought the next day would be ideal to take Bill. I seemed to have found the spot. It was, not surprisingly, a bit of a walk from the road and it appeared that a lot of the pressured birds had discovered this little oasis in the middle of the harder hit cover. I was certain I could put Bill on a bird here. Still a good sport, though our track records on birds together this season was exactly zero, Bill agreed to meet me there. I could almost guarantee we'd get a flush, I told him. The birds were *there*. The pause at the other end of the line politely signaled his doubt. Meeting at the parking lot of the small state park, Bill and the dogs greeted each other, the dogs with perhaps a bit more enthusiasm than Bill.

"What is with this heat?" I asked.

"Too early for excuses yet. Give it time."

I like Bill.

On the way back to the secret pheasant honey hole, Max started acting goofy. It didn't look quite like he was birdy. His movements weren't yet rigid and focused. I guessed that he was on very old scent. Nowhere near Max, a cackling rooster erupted from the grass behind and to the right of Bill. It was an awkward angle and he couldn't get on it quickly enough. In Bill's defense, it was an impossible shot. We watched helplessly as the rooster disappeared over a line of distant oaks.

"Too early for excuses, still?"

He laughed.

Nearing the small oasis at the back of the property, Max picked up scent again. This time he was right down to business, the circling and tracking turning into an all-out run. I told Bill to get ready. The rooster rocketed just three feet off the end of Max's jaws. He almost caught it. Though it came up in front of Bill, the bird flew across in front of me. Perhaps more concerned with Max than the two guys with shotguns, it passed me at only three or four yards before towering over a small pin-oak twenty yards out. I did the mental calculations as quickly as possible. It, too, was about to disappear. Once again, Bill had no shot. I did. The bird went down hard, and Max pounced on it with his usual skill. To add insult to injury, he dropped the pheasant at Bill's feet.

"Oh *thanks*, Max!"

He was still smiling. I recognized those writer-wheels turning.

"Sorry . . . I didn't mean to shoot it out from under you."

"That's fine! I didn't have a shot."

It was true, but I still felt bad. I'd like this to be one of those stories where our fortunes turned on a dime and Bill finally connected on a Max-flushed pheasant, but . . . no. When Bill and I finally regrouped a week later, the weather had changed. Cool nights had frosted the ground several times and the days felt less like early September and more like late October should. While I *knew* there would be birds at the state land, I didn't want to give the appearance of doing the same thing over and over again and expecting a different result. I suggested a different hunting spot. Bill agreed, perhaps a bit too enthusiastically . . .

Max covered the cold ground quickly and with more eagerness than I'd seen in a week. Even more than I, he was happy to have a reprieve from the unseasonable weather. No swims in the pond would be required to keep him hunting hard today. Bill and I walked along, talking about everything and anything. Any number of subjects might be covered in a day's hunt with Bill. I suppose that's one of the advantages to hunting with people my own age, or even a bit older. We'd fallen into the rhythm of idle chat when Max suddenly went ballistic. Darting left and right, his nose never more than a half-centimeter above the ground, I'd seen this before. It almost always ends in a flush. Still, something seemed off. He was darting *too* far left and *too* far right. He's never been much for chasing rabbits, but

I began to wonder, hoping it wasn't something more exotic, like a skunk. My worries dissolved however when two roosters burst from the cover just in front of Max, and only a few yards apart. One went up to the right, and I dropped it. The other went to the left, and Bill made an excellent passing shot. Feathers rained down in front of both of us. Max, quite unaccustomed to having to handle two birds at once, picked up one bird and carried it over to the other. Waiting patiently for us to come tell him what to do with his pile of pheasant, his tail wagged as fast as I've ever seen it go. His golden smile said, *now that was fun!* I agreed. Bill picked up the birds and handed me one of them, and we congratulated each other on our shooting. The curse had finally been broken. And we'd been hunting all of twenty minutes before the seven-ten split. I patted Max on the head and gave him a drink of water, secretly thanking him for pulling through for Bill.

Now that, I thought to myself, *is a story I'd like to see in print.*

10

WILD NORTHERN SCENES

I HAVE a few favorite hunting writers. For adventure and humor, Peter Capstick's *Death* series cannot be beat. *Death in the Long Grass* is the first and best of that series. The harrowing hunts, man-killing beasts, and black humor make me return to it frequently. It's bombastic and completely readable. Unlike many of the Victorian-era African hunting tales which tend toward stuffiness, Capstick's take is a thoroughly modern look at chasing and (sometimes unsuccessfully) removing dangerous creatures. I've read many of the lines a dozen times, but they still make me laugh out loud upon each revisiting. Perhaps my favorite line is when he calls an unfortunate death at the hands of a vicious man-eating creature *The Big Surprise*. His descriptions of cleaning up what's left of a human body after an elephant attack are not to be missed. Every sentence, no matter how bleak, is delivered with mischievous good cheer. I love Capstick's writing.

On a completely different wavelength from Peter Capstick's high adventures in the long grass and lonely lands, any modern

hunting reader's list must include Gene Hill. He was the antithesis of Peter Capstick. With a Harvard degree, he had a successful run as an advertising copyrighter for several Madison
Avenue ad agencies. He walked away from it all to start a new
life as a fulltime writer. An *outdoor writer.* Eventually becoming a long-time columnist for *Field & Stream*, Hill's tales of
dogs and deer, fishing and friends are written beauty and simple passion. Each time I read one of his books, he makes me
want to go look at one of my old guns, or a knife that a long-
since-passed hunting partner gave me. I think his career in
advertising had a direct influence on the impact of his writing.
He makes me want to pat my bird dogs on their heads and helps
me to remember that their lives are short. He knew how to sell
it. Gene Hill could say more in one paragraph than most writers can say in an entire book. His style was direct, but breezy.
Serious, yet funny. Every page of every book is a glimpse into
the man's heart. What authors struggle to do, Gene Hill managed to do so effortlessly. I suppose I shouldn't assume it was
effortless, precisely. I'm guessing a lot of tears went into those
short, concise paragraphs. Early on in my authoring career,
back when the Internet was young, an angry online reviewer
essentially said of one of my books, "This author is no Gene
Hill." That was crushing to a young writer with only two books
under his belt. I didn't want to be Gene Hill, but I didn't necessarily need to be told that the idea was hopeless, either. I've
gotten over it but, as you see, may still hold just the smallest
hint of a grudge.

I don't read a lot of hunting books these days, unless I hear
about an exceptional one, or a friend of mine writes one. I read,
but it's more often about politics or natural history. Frequently
these days, I'll go back and re-read something I know I'm going
to love. It may have something to do with the advance of old
age and the realization that, if I want to keep having adventures

enough to write about and time enough to write them, something has to give. Unfortunately, my reading of hunting literature has suffered.

In the offseason (the three days between hunting and fishing season), Joy and I often seek out local estate sales. Joy has exquisite taste and our house (other than the room that is home to a growing number of deer heads and bear rugs) is decorated with an eclectic mix of antiques, all arranged with her comfortably casual style, yet still looking as if any given table could easily grace the cover of a magazine. In our attic, for example, we found several vintage suitcases that belonged to my grandmother. Three of them stacked now serve as an end table by our living room couch. I never would have thought of that, and it looks good!

Estate sales vary in quality from the sad, musty, small houses, stripped bare of anything worth buying before the doors even open, all the way to the opulent homes owned by doctors and lawyers and other well-to-do individuals. Those homes often contain interesting pieces of furniture and artwork. One, just a few years ago, was the former home of a well-off doctor who was also an avid duck hunter and fly-fisherman. *Bingo!* Prices, as well, range from the ridiculously dreamy money people hope to get for not-very-good pieces, to sometimes reasonable prices for items such as, say, fly-tying supplies. You never know. Universally, though, you can get books at estate sales for very reasonable prices. Often, they're marked at pennies on the dollar of the original cover prices. There are often piles of commercial novels from familiar authors, like Tom Clancy, Patricia Cornwell, and the like. Sometimes there are hidden gems, like coffee-table books of wildlife photography. I don't know if you've priced any coffee-table books lately, but they're ridiculously expensive, upwards of $50 or even $100. At an estate sale? Two bucks, tops. As an author, it makes me sad to see all that hard work being sold at lower than bargain-bin prices. But, I suppose, at least the work lives on.

Seven or eight years ago, Joy and I stumbled upon a humble estate sale. The house was likely magnificent in its day, but the hardwood floors were sagging and filthy. Mildew crept up the wallpaper that hung there since the beginning of the last century. There wasn't much to be had in the way of collectibles or antiques, either. The house did contain, however, an enormous library, with books on shelves stretching from the floor to the high ceilings. Not just on the shelves, books were stacked everywhere. A large handwritten sign said, *Books $2. Three for $5.* Most of the books looked ancient. While there were some more modern titles scattered about, the majority had faded, cracked bindings and cloth covers. There were a lot of antique books on those shelves. I didn't have the patience to comb through what must have been thousands of books. In retrospect, at those prices, I should have just filled a box with a hundred bucks worth of books and gone home to see if I'd found anything good. I didn't, though. A nature book from the 1800s caught my eye. I snatched it up and leafed through the old, pen-and-ink drawings of familiar northeastern writing. It held a great deal of charm in its descriptions and sketches. I tucked it under my arm. Farther down that same shelf, I came across another title, *Wild Northern Scenes: Or Sporting Adventures with the Rifle and Rod* by S.H. Hammond. Bingo. I've read a lot of old outdoor literature and, to be honest, the dated prose often bores me to tears. Years ago (1996 according to IMDB—can that possibly be right?), after watching and thoroughly enjoying the film, *The Ghost and The Darkness,* I set about reading the book from which it was derived, *The Man Eaters of Tsavo.* I was bored to tears. *Wild Northern Scenes,* though written even thirty years earlier, was anything but stuffy. Just glancing through it in the din and clutter of the estate sale, I recognized the playfulness of Peter Capstick and the thoughtfulness of Gene Hill in this much older work. Though the writing bore the hallmarks of older prose in its non-standardized spellings and names of locations, it was a good book, well worth $2.

When I got home, I read *Wild Northern Scenes* from cover to cover before the sun had set. I was fascinated. The book is the tale of a weeks-long outdoor adventure undertaken by the author, a few friends, and several hired men. What were the hired men for? To carry the guns, row the boats, skin and cook the game, and whatever else might have been required of them. The book resonated with me on several levels, many of them having to do with the fact I hunted many of those same areas of the Adirondack Mountains in New York over the years. The author and his friends hailed from Albany, just a short train ride from the Adirondacks even back then. But their explorations and exploits took them far and wide, traversing rivers, lakes, and mountains in a still-unspoiled wilderness.

Most astounding to me in *Wild Northern Scenes* was the freedom these men enjoyed on their hunts. Although game laws have been in place since Colonial times, some hundred years prior to the book's writing, the amount of game the author and his cohorts not only saw, but killed, is staggering. It was a glimpse into a past long-forgotten. The hunters took dozens of deer, some bears, small game, ducks, and grouse. One story tells of shooting a small black animal off a ledge that plummeted into the lake below. The animal turned out to be a black-phase fox. Quite unusual then, and even today very rare. I found it telling they had no idea what they were shooting at until they'd retrieved it out of the lake. Those were the days, I suppose. On the list of animals no longer present in sufficient numbers to hunt in New York, they also interacted with and harvested mountain lions and moose. (Moose are only now beginning to reestablish breeding populations in the Adirondacks.) Though

S.H. Hammond and his friends (who called him Samuel) spent weeks shooting countless animals and catching baskets full of trout, he pointedly wrote how they never took more than they needed for camp food, which for upwards of ten men was, in fact, quite a lot. He seemed, peripherally at least, aware that they took a *lot of game*. I envied them the freedom, though the pages sometimes delved into what could most kindly be described as *gluttony*. For someone writing about hunting in 2020, it's hard to judge the mindset of someone hunting in the 1850s. Things were different then. Much different. Perhaps not coincidentally, the whitetail deer population in New York State began a precipitous plunge shortly after the writing of *Wild Northern Scenes*. Although Hammond recognized the need to preserve the wonderful, wild, vast area known as the Adirondacks, he had less to say about the need to reform game laws. Interestingly, within forty years of his writing, the Adirondack Park was designated *Forever Wild*, perhaps one of the most prescient decisions any government in modern times has ever made. Those same streams, ponds, woods, and lakes are there for our enjoyment over a century later. Despite some rough handling by timber and mining companies in the early days of their exploration, the Adirondack Mountains serve as an early example of the forethought required for good conservation practices. In the early 1900s, the game laws also underwent some radical changes, becoming more restrictive than they'd ever been. When that happened, it would still be another fifty years before Aldo Leopold's *A Sand County Almanac* would, through its informal prose, become the definitive word on conservation in 1949. Much has happened since then, as well, when it comes to preserving sustainable populations of wildlife for hunters, fishermen, and nature enthusiasts alike.

Wild Northern Scenes disappeared from my possession about five years ago. I loan out books. Sometimes they come back and sometimes they don't. I don't mind. I'm sure there are some on my shelves that belong to someone else. It happens. When John appeared one day at my door, just in from his new home in Florida, he had the tattered, faded old book in his hands. I had forgotten about it. Paging through it a few weeks before starting to write this book, I was again struck by the difference between *then* and *now.* A hundred years isn't a long time in the history of the world, but it is a long time in the history of conservation. With the theme of this book centering on thinking of the future, and the future of hunting, I found myself imagining what S.H. Hammond and his well-heeled hunting friends would think of our current game laws. I don't think it's a stretch to say that he would see the current state of hunting as terribly restrictive and wish to return to his own timeline posthaste. I've lived with these modern, evolving regulations my whole life and even I see them as unnecessarily prohibitive at times. I recognize the need to sometimes dial back consumptive use and utilize science to the best of our abilities to maintain healthy animal populations and, in turn, a robust ecosystem. Still, at times I think it would be fun to float down the Racquette River (or the *Rackett,* as Samuel called it) and hunt whatever I wanted for as long as I wanted. I'd call a few of my friends from the big city, and ask them to join me, promising only weeks of adventure and guaranteeing all the venison, trout, and ducks they could possibly want to eat. No questions asked.

Wild Northern Scenes indeed.

11

I WON'T BE HERE MUCH LONGER

I'VE SPENT a lot of time trying to comprehend time. When I read philosophy, I tend to read about things like fate, death, and time. I'm a fun guy. That's not *all* I read about, but lately it fascinates me more than ever to realize how little we know about just about anything. The older I get, the more these concepts interest me and, the more I dig specifically into time, the more I realize humans have been trying to figure it out forever. For as long as humans have put words on paper, and probably longer, time has confounded mankind. Time. What is it good for? Absolutely nothing. Say it again. I'd just completed the finishing touches on the chapter of this book called *Overbooked*. In that story from 2018, Max (with a little help from Fred) hunted an arid, hot day over five hunters and never complained, never faltered, and never slowed. Writing about my dogs (especially the good ones, which has been *all* of them) is a pleasure. I can close my eyes, think about those days in golden fields, and my fingers fly as words appear on the screen before me. *Overbooked* was no exception. Now that the chapter was done—for now, anyway—I poured a glass of wine from the big, oh-so-classy wine box on the counter and settled in before the television. Joy was already snoozing on the other end of the couch. I ran the DVR menu, trying to decide between "Jeopardy," a documentary on meerkats, or the newest "Ancient Aliens." Don't judge me, and I won't judge you, dear reader. I finally settled on a news station. I wasn't terribly interested in the latest goings-on in Washington, but it would make for good background noise as I thumbed the pages of the newest Cabela's catalog, daydreaming about the coming hunting season. Lucy, our rescue springer, was curled up at Joy's feet on the couch. Fred was finally settled in on the floor, both of his retrieving balls within easy reach. It's a rare treat—but most definitely a *treat*—to see Fred done-for. He doesn't tire easily, and it's often a blessing when he finally does. That is one high-energy springer. I like Fred.

I sipped my wine and tried to make sense of what was being relayed via the Washington correspondent. I like news. I'm a political junkie. In my old age, I've learned to realize with whom politics could be discussed. I've also discovered there are those with whom politics must *never* be discussed. I don't have the energy any longer to be an instigator. I used to be, and I miss it. I will, however, admit that I was just about done with the recent political histrionics. Cabela's was far more interesting. I made a mental side-list of things I should buy that I probably don't really need. I whittled that down to things I *want* but can't afford. The list dwindled significantly. It was just about empty, in fact. Sometime around midnight, the news droned on and Joy and the springers had retreated to the bedroom. Max normally would have joined them but stayed by my feet, warming them with his big, furry presence. I wasn't sure why. Once I've been writing, it's hard to turn off the central processor, and this evening was no exception. I was wide awake. Max seemed to sense it and awoke from his own nap. On some mysterious doggie cue, he stood and placed his head in my lap.

Golden retrievers are beautiful dogs. Their lines, their flowing coats, their expressive faces. There is nothing not to love about the appearance of a golden retriever. They are beauty in action. Before we got Max, I'd read about the issues of having a golden for a hunting dog. My own stubbornness and Max's indefatigable cuteness as a puppy, however, let the common wisdom of *not* depending on a golden retriever as your bird dog be easily dismissed. It was relegated to a familiar refuse pile containing much of the other common knowledge about bird dogs I've read over the years. Max was a natural pheasant and woodcock hunter and could hold his own on waterfowl retrieves as well, despite his lack of experience. Besides, he was fun to be around. I've had several hunting partners who were *terrible* hunters but made up for it by their knack for making me laugh. Max is anything but terrible but still makes me laugh on a regular basis. If Max has any checks in the negative column, one of them is that he tends to jump on our houseguests. Dog people recognize that he's trying to give them a hug. Non-dog people tend to look at those embraces as if they're being mauled by a rabid black bear. Both are good for amusement, especially the latter. I'm not sure why *any* non-dog people still come to our house, now that you mention it.

Max looked up at me, into my eyes, and into my soul. Unlike many gundogs I've owned, his eyes and ears are still sharp going into old age. That once-golden muzzle is now tinged with gray, those deep, intelligent eyes outlined in white. For the first time in nine years, I saw my constant companion as an old dog. Max has hunted hard since he was a puppy, and it was hard to see him slow down this past year. With a skin infection putting him out of commission for a good part of pheasant season, I hadn't seen the ravages of time exhibit themselves quite as vividly as they had the last two years. Now, though, Max looked like an old dog. I started doing the math. *He's what, 8?* No. That's not right. He was 9. Nine isn't old for a springer spaniel, but it is for a golden retriever. Goldens' lifespans are typically ten to twelve years. How is it that our puppy could already be there? I shook my head. I still don't understand time. With Max's broad head in my lap, I rubbed the gray ridge between his eyes with my index finger.

"Good boy, Max."

His tail wagged in great, slow, sweeping undulations. Reflexively, I reached for my wine glass, now almost empty. That fringed, golden tail has accounted for more spilled liquids in our house than I can even begin to tell you. The oriental rug in our great room bears the stains of many evenings' worth of wine spilled by that very tail. springers don't spill wine, except when they're trying to drink it. Their nubby tails are no good for making a huge mess. As I lunged for my glass, Max seemed to smile. Max almost *always* looks like he is smiling, but this smile had a bit of the devil in it. When we were researching buying Max nine years ago, we came across the phrase, *the smartest breed,* many times in reference to golden retrievers. Whenever Max does something smart, or dumb, or destructive, or funny, we often repeat that phrase. *The smartest breed.*

Max looked into my eyes in the quiet evening.

"Good boy."

His tail wagged faster.

Maybe it's just the hazard of walking around during the book-writing process with multiple heavy thought bubble hanging over my head, but something in Max's look caused tears to roll down my cheeks. Emotion has always been a large part of hunting season to me but, as the years roll on, it's become even more present, more persistent. Maybe—just maybe—even a little more of a problem. I saw it in my dad as he got older, and in several of my own older hunting partners. Still, its effect is undeniable. Getting old makes you more emotional. Does it work the same for dogs? Maybe. The look in Max's eyes as that big, golden tail swept the coffee table said, "Hey, you know I won't be here much longer, right?"

I love Fred. I love my hunting partners. But, for the better part of the last decade, Max has been my right hand, especially during bird season. He has made me better than I am. Max has already taken his place among the dogs I consider to be the top of the heap when it comes to hunting. His eyes said to me that night, "Don't forget about me. My time grows short." As much as dogs can be frustrating, aggravating, and any other number of adjectives that go hand in hand with sharing a house with large carnivores, they are a huge part of our lives. Not for the first time in 2019, I buried my nose and cried into Max's fur. I've been through it too many times before. This time, unfortunately, I can see it coming. Although he's still willing and able, the truth is that Max's last hunt is drawing near. He knows it. I know it. Much has been said about animals being blessed with not knowing such things. It's not true. I think, conversely, that animals *do* know that their time is limited. Their lives are concentrated, distilled down to what matters. Max knows. It's their gift. It allows them to live with intensity, enthusiasm, and purpose. We should all get just a sliver of such profound knowledge. So many people ignore it, believing this life goes on forever. Sometimes it's worthwhile to take a tentative step into the edge of that forest known as the future. It may be scary, but it can also serve as a stern reminder that our time is growing short.

Scratching the gray fur between Max's eyes once again, I sensed the approaching inevitability. I think Max did, too.

Sometimes, I hate the future.

12

ONE & DONE

THE LAST few years, in addition to my youthful hunting companions, I have hunted with people my own age, such as my brother-in-law Steve, and my friends Dave, Bill, and John. I'm always happy to share a hunt with people with whom I can actually keep up. Today, it was Scott. A salmon trolling expert, Scott shared a great day fishing with me. A year passed since then and I hoped he had forgiven me a nasty netting mishap during which I caused a twenty-plus-pound salmon to be lost at the side of the boat. If he hadn't forgotten it, he was at least nice enough not to mention it. I owed him a pheasant hunt or two, either way. Of course, the day we selected was a deluge of cold, pouring rain. On the phone the night before, after watching the forecast, I gave him an out.

"Will the dogs be able to find birds in the rain?" he asked.

"Yes."

"Then let's do it."

It was the answer I'd hoped for. I've heard other bird hunters claim that pheasants are tough to come by in the rain. I don't discourage them from their beliefs. It keeps the bird hunting areas relatively empty during inclement weather. That's fine with me, because we shoot a lot of birds in the rain.

Early on in the hunt, Max got birdy, tearing up the brush and snorting excitedly.

"Get ready. He's going to flush one."

Max didn't flush one. Oh, there was a rooster cackling and a thunderous flapping of wings. The bird made it about three feet off the ground when my trusty golden retriever *also* made it about three feet off the ground and caught the bird in mid-air. Scott and I both still had our guns up while Max dispatched the bird and dutifully retrieved it to Scott's feet.

"Does that happen a lot?" he asked.

"Sometimes. The rain slows them down a little . . . "

"Will I get to shoot one, or should I just put my shotgun back in the truck?"

I laughed. "You might. Keep the gun handy."

The rain increased from steady to intense. Bird hunting in the rain is pretty much the same as hunting on a sunny, bluebird day, except for the water. Not only does the rain coming from the sky strive to soak you, but the already-wet, waist- and chest-deep brush does a fine job of finishing you off. Transitioning from a small brushy area I hoped might hold a few woodcock, Max, Scott, and I already looked like drowned rats. The rain came down even more heavily and ran down my back under my waterproof jacket.

"This is a good field," I said cheerfully, though not feeling it.

Scott nodded and smiled.

"Get 'em, Max."

Coursing back and forth between Scott and me, the golden boy had worked half of the small, long grass field when he suddenly locked on scent. Watching the big, goofy house dog turn from amiable pet into hunting machine never fails to amaze me.

Bird scent has an effect on him that is unmistakable. Hunched down, muscles taught, switching back and forth on the scent trail to determine direction, Max on scent is a sight to behold.

"He's birdy. We need to keep up with him."

A thousand other hunts on days both rainy and sunny suggested to me this bird was going to stay just ahead of us until the end of the field, where he'd flush out through a tangle of saplings, making shooting a challenge at best. Not wanting to shoot a bird out from under Scott, I hung back just a few yards as he rushed after Max, who was closing the distance to the end of the field at a staggering rate.

"He's gonna flush," I yelled.

Scott didn't look at me but nodded. His shotgun was half up as the distance to the end of the field closed from fifty yards, to twenty, and then ten. The cackle of the bird, though not surprising, still made me jump and reflexively jerk my own shotgun up to the shooting position. *Curse these reflexes of mine.* I put the gun down. This one was Scott's, hit or miss. Just out of the grass, the bird was a low-flying rocket in the pouring rain. It tumbled at Scott's shot.

Perfect.

Max retrieved the rooster to Scott. Both Max and the bird retained none of their glorious, normal colors on this dismal, gray, wet day. Scott held the bird up for me to see, deftly swinging it out of the way when Max tried to snag it back out of his hand with a powerful vertical jump. Max does love his birds.

"Was that a professional shot or what?" he asked, admiring his first pheasant.

I had to admit it was.

"Well, that's one for Max, one for me, and now it's your turn!"

I told him he was more than welcome to shoot the next one too. He could possibly have his first bird *and* his first two-bird limit on his first day bird hunting. He laughed, saying he was just happy to get one. It doesn't always work that way with experienced *or* inexperienced hunters, and he had fought the rain and made a great shot. I was happy for him, as well.

Unplanned though it was, and almost always is, the next bird went up in front of me. It may have appeared that I paid Max off to perfectly flush a bird only I had a shot at, but in reality it just happened that way. Max *does* know who gives him the treats back home. The shot may or may not have been *professional,* as Scott might describe it, but the bird dropped. That's a good thing, because my finger was sliding all over the wet trigger guard, trying to find the second trigger. Thankfully, it wasn't needed. Max brought the bird back to me and I quickly tucked it in my vest. Overhead in the clouds an unseen, but huge, flock of migratory geese passed us. Their muted honks carried over the rain and wind.

It was a nice, if wet, autumn moment.

"One for each of us," Scott said.

We shook hands.

"I'm as wet on the inside as I am on the outside," I said.

"I'm ready when you are," Scott replied.

"Want to try to get one more?" I asked.

"No, I'm good. I'm glad to have gotten one."

Three big roosters in the vest is a pretty good hunt any day of the season. We walked slowly back to the trucks, discussing the upcoming fishing season. I told him that he was welcome to join me any other day, since I'd be off for the next week and a half with only two purposes: pike fishing and pheasant hunting.

"No, but thanks. I'm going to quit while I'm at 100 percent."

And he did just that. He never bird hunted with me again.

13

PHOTO OPS

*Everybody can be a great photographer if they zoom
in enough on what they love.*
—*David Bailey*

THERE'S SOMETHING about photography that fits like a missing puzzle piece into a writer's mind. So many of the writers I've known often have a camera (usually a *real* one) within easy reach at any given time. I suppose it's the same need to document moments and events. Every writer, no matter how humble, has enough of an underlying ego to think, *this might be interesting to someone someday.* I think the photographer's mindset is nearly identical. It's enough to enjoy the moment, but it becomes more enjoyable if you can relive that moment later or, better yet, share it with others. The heart of a writer is not vastly different from the heart of the photographer. We're all documentarians. I've carried a camera with me since I began hunting and fishing. That blossomed into a very active wildlife photography habit, which is very much like off season hunting, only legal. I often go back and revisit those thirty-year-old photos with a sad smile, wondering what happened to those young guys. In the writing of this book, I've frequently perused a file folder of scans on my computer called *Old Hunting Photos* for inspiration and a look back to the days when I was the same age as my current, much younger hunting partners. Looking at the photos from the more recent years, I probably should start a file called *Old Men Hunting Photos*.

Hunting is a messy sport, whether it's waterfowl or pheasants, woodcock or deer. It's often chaotic, unpredictable, and doesn't lend itself well to documentary photography. There's always mud, obtrusive brush, uncooperative dogs, snow, or a rainy downpour to help prevent any *real* photography occurring under what can only be described as *normal* field conditions. I love my dogs but, I'm sorry, hunting dogs are the worst photo subjects in the long, storied history of bad photo subjects. Give me a wild fox or coyote any day. They are much more likely to listen. Of all the pheasant dogs I've ever had, Max has the most elegant retrieve. Holding a pheasant fully by the body in his big golden jaws, he's tall enough that the bird is often well above the grass. He always looks very happy and very proud on his retrieves. My springers have all been good retrievers, but their retrieves tend to be a little rougher, perhaps a little more utilitarian. Fred, though young, is blossoming into a pretty good retriever. Unfortunately, his retrieving style could best be summed up as *here's your damned bird*. Once a pheasant is dropped at my feet, Fred doesn't want to pose, much less put it back in his mouth while I tell him to *hold it, hold it*. He does his duty, but not much more. Max can always be counted on for a proud pose with a hard-won bird. Fred, not so much. Along with the dogs' lack of cooperation, a real retrieve often includes sticks or saplings blocking the view and subsequently raising hell with the camera's focusing system. And that's all if I happen to be able to get the camera out of its case and up (while balancing my shotgun) before the bird is unceremoniously deposited by one dog or the other. It seldom makes for a good photo.

Enter the fake retrieve.

The photos in *Old Hunting Photos,* many of them from way back in the day of film cameras, are chock full of photos of dogs retrieving ducks, pheasants, and woodcock. All of my dogs live forever in those old photographs. In the fullness of time, I've forgotten which of those tear-jerking photos of Maggie, Ted, Minnie, Charlie, Mike, Jake, and Cagney were faked. But I can tell you this: It's probably *most of them.* Usually when the dogs bring a bird back, they're almost instantly ready to start hunting again. If you take that bird, however, and throw it back out in the brush, the dogs' natural instinct to bring it back to you once again kicks in. Sometimes I stage the fake retrieves for later in the hunt. Other times I wait until the light is a little better than when the shot actually took place. Sometimes, the retrieves take place in cover so thick that photography is nearly impossible, and that cover is exchanged for a bit more open field, where Max's pretty retrieves can be shown in all of their glory, no matter how contrived.

In addition to setting up upland retrieving shots, the other hunting sports lend themselves well to, well . . . *prepared* shots that better reflect a good take of ducks, or a nice deer than a hastily taken, poor quality phone photo could ever do. Phone photos have their place, especially when taunting your friends who are stuck at work or having a slower day hunting than you. For those rich, memorable photos to help pass the months until the season rolls around again, though, you can't beat a better camera and just a little preparation. In the opening chapter of this book, I told about hunting the frigid Lake Ontario bay for diver ducks with Porter and his friends. We returned several days to enjoy the sight of those lightning-fast little divers decoying in. On one of those arctic days, we killed a several-man limit of long-tailed ducks and one beautiful drake mallard. It was too cold to take photos as the action was unfolding. Too cold, and the shooting was too good to be bothered with photography. At the end, however, Porter carefully lined the ducks up on a boulder and we got several good shots. Porter planned to use my big fishing kayak (which he'd used to set the decoys, retrieve the ducks, and shoot the mallard) to ferry the bird haul back to the boat launch. I had an idea that it might make a good photo to have the ducks all posed on the bow of the kayak and I'd get some photos of him paddling by. Porter, rather than make a messy pile of ducks and get it over with so we could retreat to the warmth of our trucks, carefully stacked the ducks. Each had its head turned just so. The bloodier ones went on the bottom. The mallard was given a place of prominence. It was a perfect pyramid of ducks, balanced carefully on the pointed nose of the kayak. Not many people would have put that much effort into it. I appreciated it, though.

Porter's natural knack for dead-wildlife photography (I couldn't think of a better name for it) came in handy during last deer season as well. The day of the late-season muzzle-loader hunt during which he put me on the big buck and doe, we decided there was enough time to get some photos of our to-date most successful hunt together. Porter suggested that we drag the deer out of the thick woods and down into the more scenic, better-lit edge. It was a good idea. He did, however, suggest that we also not field-dress them until we'd gotten our fill of photos. That was *also* a good idea, but it made the chore of dragging two huge animals many dozens of yards that much harder due to the fact they were each carrying an extra forty or so pounds of weight. In the end, though, we got photos that were fitting tributes to the excitement of that hunt. Truth be told, we spent more time photographing than we had *shooting* the two deer. I didn't mind. Porter is one of the few people who understands that getting some good photos of a memorable day is well worth the extra effort.

My friend Dave is a professional photographer. The first time I took him on a pheasant hunt with Max, we got a couple of birds. At the end, I suggested that we fake (I really don't like that word. *Fabricate?* Same thing, I suppose, but it just sounds so *dishonest*) a few photos of Max retrieving in the long grass— which was quite a lot more scenic than the brush-choked areas where the birds had, in fact, been shot. While Dave tossed the birds into the grass, I took several sequences of Max professionally retrieving them, time and time again. Dave spun in a circle, eyeing the sky, and made a few suggestions on taking advantage of the sun's angle on the golden field. We put Max through his paces again and got some wonderful photos. As we finished up, an older hunter (yes, that's still possible!) passed us, following his GSP through the long grass. If he wondered what these two yo-yos were doing tossing a bird repeatedly out into the field, he didn't say anything.

He was old enough that I supposed he'd seen sillier things.

14

WATERPROOF

HALFWAY TO Porter's house, I began doubting my sanity. The drive takes two hours. Only an hour into the trip, I hit heavy, driving rain no fewer than five times. Between the heavy, driving rain was light, annoying rain. I never once hit a nice, clear patch. I'm not sure why I was surprised. While weather forecasts can be predictably incorrect, they'd been calling for a heavy, Monday rain for five days. Forecasters are never wrong when you want them to be. Still, if I canceled all my hunt plans because it called for rain, I'd spend a lot more time at home or in the office. No thanks.

Porter and Melody met me in the driveway. Mel was feeding the pigs and Porter was tidying up the garage. Each of them was decked out in raingear. I don't *have* any raingear. I used to wear raincoats and waterproof pants but found, early on, that I often ended up wetter on the inside than on the outside. My solution, at this late date in my hunting career, is to just bring extra clothes. On many days like this one promised to be, I brought *two* sets of clothes. Knowing this was going to be a soaker, and a soaker two hours from home, I brought three.

73

I'd met Porter's girlfriend, Melody, once before at a family gathering. She seemed quiet. Already a check in the *win* column. Seeing her here, in her natural element, surrounded by domestic ducks and geese, goats and pigs, she seemed to positively *beam,* even in the rain. I looked forward to seeing her shoot her first pheasant. I let Max and Fred out of the backseat of the truck. It took a minute to get them to stop harassing the ducks.

Earlier, Porter heard a wild rooster cackling on the hillside adjacent to their farm and suggested we start there. Crossing the slick, steep ravine, I secretly hoped we would flush a grouse. You can't find them near my house. As we plodded up the far side of the brook, the dogs coursed restlessly back and forth in the newly fallen October leaves. No grouse, and no scent. Once on top, Porter pointed out a small, brushy thicket from which he'd heard the rooster cackling. I quickly surveyed the area. Thick cover formed a wedge between the brook and a fresh-cut cornfield. Perfect.

Not having hunted the area, and perhaps feeling a bit out of sorts, it took some coaxing to get the dogs to work cover. I suspect they were distracted by the heavy presence of deer scent along the field edge, certainly more than either of them had ever experienced back home. Finally, unable to convince the dogs to work the likely pheasant cover, I went into the thick brush, up to my chest. Max dutifully followed, while Fred insisted on running the edges. *That's okay,* I thought. *He'll learn.* Into the brush and saplings, the rain had lessened a bit, but the brush dumped gallons of water down my neck and back. It was simply one of those days, in a bird hunting career full of *those days.* We plodded on. Twice, Max got on scent but quickly dismissed it. I suspected he was smelling rabbits. Porter and Mel skirted the outer edge, with Fred keeping them company. Only twenty minutes into the morning hunt, Max and I exited the far side of the thicket into the cornfield. We were both soaked. Max didn't seem to mind and, though I did, I tried my best to ignore it. We spent the next hour scouring the edges and hedgerows around the cornfield, but never put up a bird. Max once disappeared on a tear that ended in a small stand of towering white pines. While we didn't see, hear, or smell a bird, I know Max and was certain he had been on a pheasant. It wasn't far from where Porter heard the morning cackling.

Switching gears, we considered our options. When Porter suggested a place twenty minutes away, it was a hard offer to refuse. A friend of his killed multiple pheasants there and, from Porter's telling, it was hundreds and hundreds of acres of prime pheasant and woodcock territory. *Twist my arm.* A year earlier, I'd taken Porter on a hunt that started out with hours of fruitless pheasant hunting in one location that had, up until then, pro-duced several pheasants and woodcock. Porter had similarly made a two-hour-plus drive and I didn't want to send him home emptyhanded. I'd suggested we give it an hour in another loca-tion and, in less than two hours, we had three birds. Much like my day with Bill this year, just a simple change of scenery made all the difference in the world. I was hoping that would be the case this time, as well.

We pulled into the hunting area, down a steep drive, and arrived at a small state parking area in a great, sprawling val-ley. Through the rain clouds, I noted the yellow and golden hillsides. If it hadn't been pouring, it would have been beauti-ful. It was beautiful in its own way, but the photographer in me made a note to come back when the sun was shining, and before those leaves fell. I also noticed the entire valley was very swampy. Since we were all soaked and it was raining anyway, I didn't think a little swamp walking would make much differ-ence one way or the other. The dogs, already wet and stinking up the truck cab, certainly wouldn't mind.

It took a mile or two of wet switchgrass, slogging through a few inches of water, before the first pheasant went up. Porter encouraged Mel to shoot. Then they both shot. Then I joined in. It was pretty ugly. *Well, you can't get them all,* I thought as the bird departed for parts unknown. Finally reaching a small stand of poplars, Max got on scent and flushed a bird that Mel dropped. Her first pheasant. In the pouring rain and soaking brush, I snapped a couple of quick photos of them, while Max and Fred jumped excitedly at the bird. I think Melody and Porter were equally excited. I was too.

A few hundred yards later, a bird went up off Max's nose in an extremely sparse patch of the field. The flush caught all of us with our pants down. Porter got on the bird, but a moment late. At the shot, it wavered in flight and then went down into another small stand of poplars. Max was on the scent immediately and I could clearly hear his frustrated snorts and grunts as he tried to locate the bird. I'd marked where it went down but, obviously, it hadn't stayed there. We worked back and forth through the thick cover repeatedly, knowing the bird had to be *somewhere.* Max excels in catching escaped pheasants, and I had faith he would bring Porter his bird. Fred checked back with me over and over again, his frantic eyes searching mine. *What happened?* I didn't know. We've had a few birds run off over the years, but Max is more talented than most bird dogs I know in ensuring that does not happen. Max worked the same small patch over and over. I began kicking at brush, thinking the bird must be *right there.*

Suddenly, the rooster cackled at the far side of the small poplar thicket and there was the thunderous flapping of wings, then . . . nothing. We all exited the swampy thicket onto the main tractor path, from which it sounded like the ruckus had emanated. Across the trail, a small strip of thick thorn bushes gave way to a deep drainage ditch. The rooster cackled again and our guns all went up in unison. But, again, nothing. Suddenly a loud splash forty yards out gave way to yet another cackle. I ran down the trail, with Porter and Mel just behind me, in time to see Fred—*Fred!*—swim out into the deep ditch and grab the pheasant, still flapping, and execute a perfect water retrieve. Fred, as far as I knew, had never retrieved *anything* from the water, but he snatched that pheasant as if he were a purebred black Lab and it was a drake mallard. It was a beautiful sight to see, and my heart swelled with pride. Max, quite unused to Fred stealing any of the spotlight, rushed to snatch the pheasant back from him but Fred was having none of it. Max may have flushed it, Porter may have shot it, but that was his bird. It took a few minutes of coaxing for him to give it up. Even then, he was protective of it until the bird was finally stuffed into the back of Porter's vest.

We flushed a couple more birds. The rain came down harder now, but it was difficult not to be in good spirits with so many firsts under our belts during that one, rainy afternoon. One rooster flushed wild, and no one could get a shot off before it disappeared over a deep creek and into the inaccessible brush on the other side. A hen went up within easy shooting range, but we didn't shoot it, having agreed to only shoot roosters. While I like to encourage conservation of wild birds, after the hard hunt in the rain, I can't say my trigger finger wasn't just a bit itchy when the hen erupted from the brush only five yards from me.

When time ran out, and we all decided we should exit this rainy day to handle our real-life obligations, we began working up the long tractor path. I hung back to get some photos of Porter, Mel, and the dogs walking out ahead of me in the rain. It had been a good day. Suddenly, Max dashed off the path to the left and put up a woodcock. Porter and Mel unloaded on it but didn't connect. Circling back around, it passed me on the other side of the deep drainage ditch from which Fred had expertly retrieved the pheasant. Knowing that shooting it would mean one or all of us having to traverse the thigh-deep creek, I shot anyway. *That's why we're here, isn't it?* The woodcock went down in the chest deep sawgrass on the other side. The dogs hadn't seen it fall and were at least seventy yards away when it dropped. I signaled Max and Fred across the creek. They swam easily across but, despite my pointing, couldn't locate the bird in the sea of grass. I waded across the creek. When the cold water spilled into the top of my knee-high boots, I was neither shocked nor surprised. Well, the coldness may have *shocked* me a bit, but I'd long since ceased any semblance of *dry.* Before I could stop them, Porter and Mel slogged across as well, laughing the whole way as the icy water lapped at their legs. *What the hell,* I thought, *it's not like we're not already wet.* It took a few moments to find the woodcock. Once located, Fred pranced proudly around with it, memories of dozens of *good boy!* fresh in his mind from his heroic water retrieve. *He may be getting the hang of this,* I thought. We stood in the sawgrass talking for several moments. I don't think anyone was in a hurry to cross back over the creek to get back to the truck. Looking down the valley, now even more socked in with gray clouds, I was in no hurry to be anywhere else at all. It had been a good day bird hunting.

15

THE F-BOMB

I'VE HAD some very good dogs. That's not quite right, though. I've never had a dog that I didn't think was *very good*. Some of them were naturals, while others took a little time to come into their own. For someone who's written tens of thousands of words about bird hunting with dogs, I can't claim to be an expert. I'm not. I've never paid much attention to breeding, much to the dismay of the *serious* bird hunters I've known. My training regimen is simple: I use positive reinforcement to encourage the predatory behaviors that hunting breeds are born with. It's simple, and it's how I've done it since day one.

Right now, Max, is my number one dog. Of all the dogs I've owned (or who have owned me), Max is in a solid tie for number two with Ted, a black Lab whom I adored. Number one is still Maggie, not only because she was my first bird dog, but because she was a natural-born hunter. At the time I got Maggie, I knew nothing about training dogs and even less about pheasant hunting. Half springer, half Brittany, Maggie was a bit schizophrenic. She never fully embraced her pointing nor her flushing roots. She was a rangy dog, often flushing pheasants well out of range. The pointer blood was strong in her, but she never got that whole *pointing* thing, either. She had the range of a pointer without the discipline. I often yelled my lungs out for her on a normal day hunting. At the same time, she was also quite capable of working closely (if she felt like it) and flushed enough pheasants and woodcock *within* range to keep my hunting partners and me happily shooting away. Though she was a verified half-breed, I think a third breed may have been present as well. I believe she was part beagle. Maggie was just as happy flushing and retrieving rabbits as she was pheasants. Many bird dog owners shun the practice of *running fur,* but I really had no choice with Maggie. She was an equal opportunity hunter. Therefore, we ate a lot of rabbit. In the late season, I'd often run her with my friends' beagles and her specialty, especially in the deep snow, became catching rabbits flat-footed. That little dog was all heart. I even had her retrieving wood ducks during one early-season pond hunt many years ago. It was as if she'd been doing it her whole life. Maggie could do it all, but she was nothing if not a difficult dog, at times. The day she flushed a raccoon (assuming, I guess, that it was just a big rabbit) and rolled down the field with it, until I pulled her away and was forced to shoot it at point-blank range, took five years off my life.

Her counterpart, Ted, was also an excellent hunter and a much easier dog to control, but he spent most of his life in the shadow of Maggie. A solid, friendly, laid-back dog, he had all the best attributes of a black Lab, but was regularly outgunned by Maggie, due in most part to her ridiculous lack of self-control. Ted was the better dog, while Maggie was a more successful hunter. On the rare days when I left Maggie home, Ted was a powerhouse. As much as I loved Ted, it was hard not to compare him with Maggie. In Ted's defense, I never had to yell for him.

Like Ted, Max is not difficult at all. He readily rides in the truck, curled up quietly in the backseat on his way to hunt, unlike any other dog I've known, who typically pace, pant, bark, and paw at me until we arrive at our hunting field. Once in the field, watching Max work is a thing of beauty. With his long legs, he courses the fields with much less effort than my springers. He covers ground quickly, works closely and often out-thinks running birds into flushing. Once a successful shot is made, watching him carrying a large rooster against the autumn backdrop of golden fields and red leaves is a living work of art. Those are the days my summertime dreams of autumn are made of. Max is a good dog. With a typical goofy golden retriever personality, he's nearly human at times, but deadly serious when on bird scent. In that way, he's my modern version of Ted; a nice, fun dog, with an excellent knack for finding pheasants and woodcock. He's not adept at rabbits, though he's flushed a few. I think he doesn't like to waste his time *running fur* when there are plenty of birds to be flushed. Max is smart and proves it on a regular basis. Whenever I doubt Max's instincts or, more foolishly, his nose, it's to my own detriment. A couple of years hunting with Max reinforced that which I already knew: *Trust the dog.*

I trust Max.

And then, there's Fred. When Max turned five, we decided to get another dog, ostensibly to learn the trade. I've always liked to have two dogs working as a team. With the overlap of owning two together, I can trace a line of hunters that learned from each other, starting way back with Maggie. Following my early pattern of having a big retriever and a small flusher, we looked for a springer. Fred came to us as a cute, little eight-week-old bundle of . . . joy. Okay, sure. *Joy.* Why not? He was cute, I'll give him that. That probably helped him survive those first few months.

I've never had a problem housebreaking dogs (my hunting dogs have all been house dogs). Other than the occasional pile of poop or large puddle on the floor, they've mostly house-trained very quickly. And then, as I mentioned, there's Fred. Fred did not housetrain easily. For a very long time, I was pretty sure that Fred was never going to housebreak at all. I've never been a big fan of crating dogs, though I know it is rec-ommended by serious trainers. Much like my training style, I just like to encourage the good and discourage the bad when it comes to housebreaking. It's worked very well with all my dogs, except Fred. As the weeks passed, it became apparent Fred was going to need to be a crated dog, at least for a while. He did not easily grasp the concept of going outside to do his business. Oh, don't get me wrong, he would go outside and do his business but, if he happened to be on the inside, he'd just as soon do it there. He didn't get it.

For such a high-energy, happy puppy, I *hated* to crate him. I just don't like crating. But when it came down to crating or coming home to a house full of poop, that was the only option. You know the old adage about a dog not defecating where he sleeps, which is an integral part of the whole crating philoso-phy? Yeah, well . . . Fred didn't mind crapping where he slept. Joy and I ended up setting up a *large* crate for him. First, to give him a little room and second, to give him a clean corner in which to sleep—after he pooped in his crate. I usually got home from work first and, after carrying Fred (often at arm's length) outside, I'd give him free run of the house. The prob-lem was, however, if you turned your back on Fred for two seconds, he would destroy something. I guess I've lucked out in my long line of dogs that the only truly destructive one I ever had was my first golden retriever when I was a young kid, Monty. Monty ate everything. Socks. Steel wool. I can't tell you how many trips to the vet Monty had. While Fred never really *ate* anything in his destructive phase (I'm glad now that I can call that period a *phase* because, at the time, I thought it would never end), he did destroy a lot of things. His specialty was dog beds and, as you may know, dog beds are not cheap. To put a positive spin on it, though, Fred did help us discover a source of slightly more affordable dog beds. He also chewed the edge off an oriental rug that had been in Joy's family for a long time.

Oops.

When he got slightly bigger, Fred learned he could move his crate around the hardwood floor by banging on the sides of it. He deftly slid it across the floor, got within reach of one of the other dogs' beds, and proceeded to either get a corner of it pulled into his crate to chew on it or, on two occasions, empty almost all of the stuffing into the crate. Very often, when I got home during those very trying months, I'd be greeted by a sea of brown stuffing spread all around our dining room. That's to say nothing of the crate full of pee and poop.

Our patience was wearing thin. Very thin.

It was around that time that Joy began referring to our cute little springer boy as *The F-Bomb*. It was an apt description. I'm not proud to say that the f-bomb was often dropped when coming home to the latest carnage created by our cute little puppy. From experience, I knew a lot of bad dog behavior was simply a result of boredom. Fred was (and is) a high-octane dog and spending eight hours in a crate was simply too much for him. In some ways I didn't blame him. I wouldn't want to be crated for eight hours either. I finally came up with an idea to help him get through his day. We'd put him out in our great room, where there are low windows and he could at least watch birds, squirrels, and the occasional jogger passing by. Hopefully, giving him something to look at would help ease his mind and soothe his destructive tendencies until we got home from work. With the crate wedged in the corner of two walls, next to the windows, it would be very difficult to move, as well.

It was worth a shot.

For a couple of days, the experiment seemed successful. Fred didn't destroy anything, partially because there was nothing he could reach. He even seemed to slowly get the knack of relieving himself outside, with only the occasional accident in the evening and only if he was ignored for too long. Things were looking up. And then one day, on a hot summer afternoon, I came home and . . . well . . . let's just say the f-bomb flew freely that day.

Fred was in his crate. Somehow, he flipped it completely over on its side. The wall and window up to the left of the crate were smeared with dog crap. The wall up to the right was smeared with slightly different-colored dog crap. There was dog barf on the wood floor and the puppy inside the crate? He was smeared with all of it. I don't know what must have transpired to cause that level of carnage, but it couldn't have been good. Max and Lucy stood in the opposite corner looking at me as if to say, *"Oh man, you shoulda been here."* I can only imagine what they witnessed that day.

I tried to figure a way to carry the crate out to the garden hose with Fred in it, so I didn't have to touch him. I'm not squeamish and have lived with dog crap my whole life but . . . *damn*. I couldn't figure it out and, besides, it wouldn't have mattered. The crate itself was impregnated with liquid poop and dog barf. I changed into some old clothes, letting Fred stay in the crate a few more minutes while I cooled down. It was for his own safety, if nothing else. Finally grabbing him by the poop stained collar, I dragged him outside, leaving brown streaks across the wood floor as he went. Once at the hose, I kept my calm, rinsing him down as thoroughly as is possible without soap. Chunks of nastiness came out of his horribly discolored fur. For Fred, he was remarkably stoic, possibly relieved that I didn't kill him. Once the initial *rinse* was done, I picked up the shivering pup, soaking myself in the process and carried him directly to the bathroom tub. We were in there a long time.

That fall, Fred flushed a few birds. Mostly, he followed Max around but, from time to time, got on scent all on his own and put birds up. He turned out to be a good hunter, after all. I hadn't seen him retrieve anything, because Max takes such pride in bringing back birds, he wasn't about to let the kid join in. At home in the yard, with Max safely in the house, he did a fine job retrieving the birds I tossed into the grass for him. He also housebroke rather easily after that last episode, possibly fearing that his life depended on it.

Fast-forward a year, and Fred became a proficient hunter. Working *with* Max instead of harassing him, they developed into the cadence of a veteran hunting team. I took them out in the early woodcock season several times and was very pleased. With Max beginning to slow down with the onset of middle age (much like myself), Fred filled in the gaps, working the tight brush at a fever pitch that only springers know.

Sometime just before pheasant season, Max developed a skin infection. I've had dogs with these infections before, usually just under the ears, and they came and went relatively quickly. Known as *hotspots* in the dog world, they're usually the result of wet ears, followed by a bacterial infection. The vet will tell you dogs are more likely to get them if they get wet. Hunting dogs are almost always wet. Ted used to get them, small quarter-sized spots of bare skin under the ears. Max, on the other hand, got the worst case of hotspots I've ever seen. His spread down his cheeks, up onto the top of his head, down his shoulders, and even onto his hips. He looked terrible. I got two pheasant hunts out of Max before the infections became so nasty that he required a trip to the vet. The vet gave him some meds and took him off active duty, less than one week into bird season.

Of course, I thought. *This is just my luck.*

Well, since we'd brought Fred into the fold as our future franchise quarterback, it was time to put him to work. He did okay in the late season last year and, in the last few days, had shown a real knack for finding birds—especially ones in the thick brush where Max couldn't easily go. Though I'd miss Max, it was a good opportunity to see how our number-two dog could do on his own.

Enter The F-Bomb.

Joy and I worked down one of the best pheasant fields I've ever hunted. The day I took my pal Scott out for his first (and only!) bird, I brought him here. This would be the perfect place for Fred to show us what he had. The little springer who tirelessly busted brush and leapt through the long grass alongside Max here just a week ago, putting two pheasants in the game bag was, unfortunately, nowhere to be found. To say that Fred *cowered* in that field is not an exaggeration. Frequently checking back with Joy and me, Fred never ventured more than ten yards out ahead of us. Never, at any point, did he do anything that looked like bird hunting. No checking the ground for scent, no bounding through the field, and none of the joyfulness that Fred had always exhibited with soft earth under his feet, since he was a tiny puppy. I can only attribute it to his being completely freaked out by Max's absence. In retrospect, it does seem like he was looking for Max the whole time. I was exasperated. I've since put the day in my distant memory bank, but Joy tells me I was muttering, *"This is not good . . ."* all morning. I'm sure I was. With a week and a half off for pheasant hunting, this was *not* the way I wanted to start it—with a dog that wouldn't hunt.

I was distraught. *What happened to my dog!?*

The next day, I took Fred out alone on a blustery, snowy hunt. Less tentative this time, he seemed to quickly understand Max was not coming. He didn't spend much time checking back with me, or looking for Max. Twice, he got on scent and ran downfield in chases that ended in no flushes. I wasn't surprised. The ability of pheasants to hide in the grass under snow cover makes that kind of hunt difficult even for very experienced dogs. The bird scent, or whatever kind of scent it was, gave Fred focus, and reminded him why he was here. The third time he got on scent he immediately flushed a beautiful rooster pheasant. Rocketing up into the blowing snow, he was flying fast on the wind. I didn't give him a chance, dropping the bird as quickly as I could. I didn't want Fred to lose *his* bird. He retrieved the rooster, at first holding it by its head in the manner that young dogs tend to do. A moment later, he dropped it, readjusted, and picked it up by the body, delivering it perfectly into my outstretched hand. Visions of my little Maggie passed through misty eyes. More of that mushy, old-guy emotion. Argh.

It's okay. I don't mind.

In the coming weeks, Fred would start proving himself as the dog of the future, as he got bolder, more confident, and refined what promised to be a great nose for birds. We've slowly switched from calling him *The F-Bomb* to the more endearing term of *The Fred Bomb*. Either one works.

Sometimes, we just call him Fred.

16

INTO THE GREAT WIDE OPEN

I'm not exactly a guy who makes new friends easily.
—Tom Petty

A WEEK after memories of the miserable, rainy-day hunt had melted away and only good memories remained, I thought again about that day in the valley with Porter and Melody. Specifically, I remembered those golden hillsides and long grass fields from which we'd flushed our birds. Wanting as much to get some photos of those hillsides in the sunlight as much as I hoped to get some more birds, I sent Porter a text.

"I want to head down there Monday, again. It looks like the sun is supposed to shine."

"Sorry, I can't. Working."

It's easier to tolerate a two-hour drive to hunt if there's someone to meet you there. I wasn't against doing it myself, but the enthusiasm for the road trip quickly waned. If I was going to hunt alone, it wasn't as if we couldn't find birds around home.

I was disappointed and, as the hours went on, I made tentative plans to hunt nearer to home. Max, still healing from his skin infection, wouldn't be able to go. And Fred had not yet proved himself a dependable solo hunter, though he was beginning to show the signs. Maybe it wouldn't be smart to gamble on him for a road trip quite yet.

A few hours later, another text came in from Porter.

"Mel wanted me to ask if she could go with you."

"Of course!"

I didn't know Melody very well yet, having met her only twice now, but she seemed like a good sport, considering the bad weather we had endured on the previous hunt. Driving down, I didn't know what to expect. While taking someone new hunting and spending hours and miles alone with a new partner isn't far off the beaten path for me, I still wanted things to go well. With Fred curled up on the backseat, much as he'd learned to do from Max's exemplary truck behavior, I pondered the possibilities of a hunt with my new partner, absent Porter to act as a buffer. I'd raised a couple of young women and, without too much forethought, I figured I could handle it. I just didn't want things to go badly, which they sometimes do on any given day during hunting season.

Meeting Melody at the same valley parking area, an old concrete pad where a barn once stood, we surveyed the sprawling horizon. Unshrouded in clouds, it was a landscape photo waiting to happen. The far hillsides lined the valley. The golden and reddish leaves, muted and partially hidden by clouds on our last trip, now blazed in all of their fiery glory. The great grass fields in the valley glowed golden yellow. Even Fred, with his happiness at being released from the truck after the long ride, seemed to pause and take it in.

Mel thanked me for letting her come and gave me a hug. I thanked her for joining me.

"It's beautiful, today," she said.

"You took the words right out of my mouth."

Getting first things out of the way first, I warned her that I would probably be taking a lot of photos, adding, perhaps a bit hesitantly, that I usually take photos of my hunting partners as well . . .

"Sure!"

We'd only walked a few hundred yards across a dry grass field when a hen pheasant erupted from the grass. I didn't want to shoot the bird out from under her, and didn't really want to shoot a hen, anyway. When the bird vanished down into the creek bottom, I said, "You know, I don't mind if you shoot hens."

"I'm okay with just roosters."

That's a lot of discipline for someone who's only ever shot one bird, I thought. The way my finger had settled mischievously on the trigger as the bird flushed, I wasn't sure *I* had that much discipline. Had I been there alone, that hen may have ridden back to the truck in the back of my vest.

"Roosters it is!"

Mel paused here and there, watching Fred work, appearing lost in thought. As if reading my mind, she said, "Don't mind me if I'm quiet. It's just so beautiful here. I'm trying to take it all in."

"Me too."

We covered more than a mile without another flush, though Fred acted as if he was on scent once or twice. Deeper into the valley, we cut down a wide tractor path that provided dry footing between a swamp and another large drainage ditch. I didn't expect to find birds on the path, rather figuring it was a good way to get to where we saw birds the other day without getting completely soaked. Only partway down the trail between the field we'd been hunting and bottom land we wanted to hunt,

I spotted a bright red rooster head peeking out of the grass
on the side of the trail a hundred or more yards ahead of us.
I pointed it out to Mel just as the bird ducked back into the
narrow strip of grass. Had Max been there, he would have
recognized my excitement and raced down the trail, probably
flushing the bird out of range. Fred wasn't yet tuned in to my
body language to that degree. He trotted along ahead of us,
poking at the odd patch of grass or piece of brush as we went.
As we neared the place where the bird was hidden, I motioned
Mel to hang back. I misjudged by fifteen or twenty yards but,
when Fred located the scent, he plunged into the long grass like
a bulldozer. The rooster cackled loudly for a moment but did
not flush. I thought briefly that Fred may have caught it. A split
second later, though, it rocketed out on Mel's side of the path,
crossing the big drainage ditch. It looked as if it was going to
make a clean getaway, just as Mel's shotgun roared. The bird
crumpled into the wet, swampy grass on the other side of the
creek. Much like my woodcock shot the other day, this would
take a bit of doing to retrieve. Mel and I high-fived, anyway. I
took a few tentative steps into the ditch before realizing that,
while the last one may have been three feet deep, this one was
more like five. If Max had been there, he might have swum
across and brought the bird back to us. Fred, however, hadn't
seen it go down and, despite his water prowess the other day, I
thought the blind retrieve in the long grass might be a bit much
to expect of him. We marked the spot by a small double sapling
nearby. We'd continue hunting down the path until we found a
crossing, and then hunt back up the other side and hopefully
retrieve the bird. Mel didn't seem entirely pleased about leaving her bird, but there wasn't much choice. I wasn't too pleased
either, hoping we'd ultimately be able to recover the bird.

We hurried down the tractor path more quickly now, more
in recovery mode than hunting. Likely due to our change in

mindset, we missed two more rooster pheasants sitting in the trail in front of us. Fred, Mel, and I all spotted them at the same time. While Melody did an admirable job *trying* to keep up with Fred, I didn't keep up with anyone, not for lack of trying. One of the birds flushed wildly out of range and the other pulled a vanishing act, as they're sometimes wont to do. We worked the area feverishly but couldn't find the second bird. With only a few feet of cover on each side of the path, there wasn't enough room for it to truly vanish. Surely, even Fred's inexperienced nose would find it. It may have flushed out the other side while the other bird departed, and we simply missed it. We'll never know.

Finally reaching a culvert spanning the ditch, we quickly crossed to the other side. The grass was a few inches deep in water in places but for the most part dry. Although the cover was chest deep, we were all hurrying. Even Fred seemed to know we were going back for the bird, bouncing quickly along ahead of his human companions. I suggested to everyone, including myself, that we slow down a bit and work this grass carefully. It looked like very good bird cover. It also would help Fred, I reasoned, to find the downed bird if we weren't racing along. Reaching the double sapling, I signaled to Mel that she and I should stay put while Fred worked the grass. For five minutes or better, he didn't get on scent of any kind. Doubt began to creep into my head. Had we mis-marked the spot? For the tenth time, I looked at the distinct double poplar sapling. *No, this is the spot.* The other option was the bird hit the ground running, which Porter's bird had done the other day, causing the dogs and their people several moments of heartburn until Fred straightened the situation out with his water retrieve. Mel and I walked another twenty yards, letting Fred thoroughly work the next bit of grass. Mel stayed by the drainage ditch while I moved farther into the deep grass with Fred. Suddenly, Fred

bounded frantically from side to side, up and down. I wondered if the bird *was* alive. It wasn't, but he had located it, just
a few yards off where we'd marked it. Now, only on his second
or third solo hunt, my heart beamed with pride when my pup
emerged from the grass with the pheasant gripped firmly in
his panting jaws. As if he *knew* what I wanted him to do, Fred
turned away and trotted the bird over to Melody, handing it to
her as perfectly as if it was his thousandth retrieve, rather than
his fifth or sixth. Melody and Fred posed together with their
bird underneath a perfect deep blue sky with the backdrop of
colorful autumn hills illuminating the day. I'm not sure which
one of them looked prouder. It was a close contest, and I was
right there with them.

We didn't find any more birds, unless you count the woodcock Fred flushed over my head. It wasn't a hard shot, until I
tripped backward on a poplar root as I lifted the shotgun to
fire. I was able to get the shot off, however ugly. Of course, no
woodcock were injured in the taking of that shot.

On the way out, Melody asked if I had any kids.

"Well, you know about Jennifer. My older daughter Jessica
and her husband and son live about a half-hour from us."

"Her son? You are a grandfather?"

"Easy, now."

"I mean, you don't look like you're old enough to be a
grandfather."

"Haha! Good save."

"A grandfather," she repeated, mulling it over.

"Don't push it, *kid*."

She laughed. At that moment, under fresh, cool autumn
skies, I knew I'd found a new hunting partner. Mel and Fred
hunted the trail ahead of me with renewed enthusiasm, back
toward the truck. I watched the young dog and my new young
hunting partner work the path to the road. I stood back for a

moment, as Melody might say, *taking it all in.* What I saw was more than hunters on a path. I saw more than my new dog and yet another new friend.

I saw the future.

17

DOG TIRED

*I was a dog in a past life. Really. I'll be walking down
the street and dogs will do a sort of double take, like,
hey, I know him!*
—*William H. Macy*

IF I had a chance to engage God in a two-way conversation, rather just in a one-way prayer, there are many things I would ask Him. My first questions would be about the mysteries of life, death, and time. I suspect the resultant answer may not satisfy me, though I suppose God is capable of making a pretty good case. The very next thing I would ask Him is about the lives of dogs. *Why are they so short?* I've troubled over this one for most of my adult life. The problem is that my adult life has seen the comings and goings of too many of these wonderful creatures. I hope God has a really good answer for that one, as well.

Fred is asleep on the floor in front of the fire, curled up with but not quite touching Max. Two years old now, he's blossomed into a wonderful hunter. While Max lies still and silent, Fred's feet twitch in unison, running after birds in his sleep, I assume. It was another good day in the field with Fred flushing and retrieving two pheasants for Melody and me. I was thrilled that Fred performed so well. While Joy and Lucy snoozed on the couch, Max and Fred by the fire, I sat in front of the computer screen, trying to come up with some notes that would remind me of the day. Plunking them out in the typical haphazard way in which most of my days in the field are recorded, I laughed. It wasn't anything approaching *writing,* in any formal sense of the word, but the key phrases were there. *Cool day. Fred on fire with pheasant scent. Mel and I both shot, both missed, and both got birds. Nice conversations with Melody. Fun in the sun.* At the end of each season, I print the notes and put them in a three-ringed binder. When I'm ready to write, I page through the notes, sometimes smiling at the memories as if seeing them for the first time. I grabbed the binder with the last few years' notes and thumbed through the bird-season entries, when Fred was first coming into his own as a bird dog. Though it hasn't been a great few years in the woodcock cycle, I realized after poring through the Fred notes that he's flushed more than his fair share of timberdoodles. All the springers I've had shared a similar flair for woodcock. It's not that the big dogs haven't, but springers are just *made* for slinking though the dense, low cover that woodcock prefer. Combined with the springers' relentless nature, that makes them the perfect woodcock dogs. Well, they aren't *pointers,* so I suppose they aren't *perfect,* but hunting woodcock with flushing dogs is an adventure all its own. It is, at the very least, an adventure in snap-shooting. Most of our woodcock are incidentals during pheasant season, but we usually manage a few days of woodcock-only hunting when pheasant season has not yet begun. Looking through last year's pages, I stopped at a lone, short entry: Dave & Keith. Fred's first woodcock and my first *woodcock to the face—there's a first!* I'd forgotten about Fred's first two woodcock flushes.

Dave and Keith and I already had taken two pheasants when Fred, still a very wiry little puppy, got on scent and rushed into a small dogwood thicket. Still wired from the pheasant shooting, we expected another big bird to come up. A bird came up, but it wasn't big. The woodcock rocketed out of the far side of the thicket before any of us could get our guns on it. One of the delights of chasing woodcock is that you can, well, *chase* them. Unlike pheasants who, at a missed shot, will put as much countryside between you and them as possible, woodcock rarely go much more than fifty yards. Very often it's much less than that, in the neighborhood of twenty or thirty yards. Given their explosive flushes and erratic flights, misses are quite common, so the opportunity to go in for a second (or even third) flush often saves the day. This bird was no exception. Making a wide arc around the dogwood stand, the bird plopped down in a small poplar thicket, only thirty-five yards away. I saw him go in. Fred didn't, so I called him over and put him into the wiry gray saplings. He didn't so much get birdy as he *stepped on* the bird. The woodcock had only one escape route, thanks to a large multiflora rose bush on the opposite side. He had to fly back out the way he had come in. The thing is, I was standing there. To say I was shocked when the timberdoodle brushed my cheek and forehead is not an overstatement. Had I been quicker, I might have been able to grab the bird with my free hand. I think Keith and Dave were so surprised at seeing me trying to duck out of the way that their guns never came up. This time, the woodcock disappeared back into the thicket beyond the dogwood, in cover so thick even Fred didn't want to follow.

"It hit my face!"

They were laughing.

I looked over at Fred, now older and a bit more seasoned, and laughed quietly about my notes. It never happened before and has never happened since. It was a fleeting, small moment in time but, after all, aren't those fleeting once-in-a-lifetime moments the reason we keep coming back? Fred padded along quietly in his sleep, dreaming, I presume, about birds.

be just so thrilled to see you when you get home that they make

18

BE LIKE FRED

FRED'S DESTRUCTIVE and excretory tendencies, which I detailed
in the *F-Bomb* chapter, are, thankfully, a thing of the distant,
smelly past. He's gradually turning into a dog that enjoys sitting with us on the couch and watching television, at least for
a moment or two before he bounds off to find a ball we can
throw for him. His indoor sport is chasing the ball down the
cellar stairs. The throw is made easily from the couch and, if
you don't put an end to it in a reasonable amount of time, you
could throw your arm into a painful case of tendonitis. Fred
would chase that ball all day, all night, and into the next morning, left to his own devices. He's recently discovered that if he
drops the ball at the top of the stairs, he doesn't even need us.
It's new to him, but I wouldn't be surprised if the technique is
soon perfected. Springer spaniels love their exercise.

Fans of golden retrievers often refer to them as the *most
human* of all the domestic dogs. I'm guilty of anthropomor-
phizing Max, to be sure. It's hard not to. With that adorably
expressive face, high-level intellect, and a playful bark that

very closely mimics a human voice, it's easy to think of him as a person. The truth is, Max (along with many other dogs) is *better* than a human being. Dogs have a high tolerance for boredom, are not easily angered, and tend to operate on simple principles. Most importantly, I think, dogs are the most forgiving creatures in our lives. Much more so than humans. They can spend a day locked in the house, possibly resenting you for abandoning them to go to work (I'm quite sure they *don't* understand how their dog food and toys are paid for), but then be just so thrilled to see you when you get home that they make you feel like the most important person in the world. The forgiveness is instant and expected. All of our dogs are like that, but Max is the most open about it. He simply *loves* to see you when you finally come home.

And then, there's Fred.

Fred loves to see you too, but he's a bit more selfish in that *you* being home means that *he* will get let out to play in the yard for an hour or so before dinner. He'll wag his nubby little tail, and maybe even bark in excitement, but then it's off to the backyard squirrel races.

When I was younger, I did believe that Labs and golden retrievers were the most human of dogs. But my perspective was a youthful one and I now realize that it's doing a disservice to them to compare them to humans. Advancing into my fifth decade, I must admit that I've seen more pure and good dogs than pure and good people.

Springers are farther down the evolutionary order than the big retrievers. I tend to think of spaniel behavior as very fox-like. They tend to be high-energy, impulsive, and intensely loyal to their pack and their people. And, importantly to me, they are hunters of the highest order. Spaniels are also a bit quicker to anger and, from time to time, bite the hand that feeds them. They are not far removed from their small, truly predatory cousins. While they make fine house pets (once they are housebroken!), spaniels tend to be a bit more selfish, and a bit more cat-like in their moods and behaviors. This is not a slap at spaniels. I have intensely loved every one I've ever known. It's just an observation which concludes in my recent realization that spaniels are much more like humans than the retrievers.

Spaniels aren't perfect, but they try.

Fred likes to spend the day in our great room, high on the back of the couch, enjoying the 180-degree view of the woods, yard, and garden. We recently got a new couch and there's already a Fred-sized depression on the back of one of the cushions that looks remarkably like the dent in the couch we just replaced. While Max and Lucy are generally content to sleep the day away in—you know—*dog beds,* Fred isn't. He doesn't want to miss anything happening outside. A few years ago, I spent several weeks photographing a fox den on my neighbors' property. The adults and pups often sat on top of the dirt mound, observing their territory. Fred's couch pose is remarkably similar to theirs. If I had to come up with a description of springers, I think it would be safe to say that they very much resemble an unholy combination of human *and* fox traits. And that's not necessarily a bad thing.

Arriving home from work, I let the three dogs out. While Max and Lucy warmly greet me before doing their business, Fred generally sprints out around them and makes several high-speed laps around the yard before pausing to pee on something he probably shouldn't be peeing on. Fred, since he was a troublesome puppy, employs a manner of running that, if it doesn't make you smile, you may not have a beating heart. Pounding the ground with his front feet, he leaps almost as high in the air as the distance he covers moving forward. He'll throw his head around, grabbing any nearby stick as a toy as he races about.

Every bone in his body and every hair on his coat signals *I am just so happy to be alive!*

He's simply a joy to watch.

In the pheasant fields, he has the endearing springer trait of making great vertical leaps to locate his people. Making up for their short legs, it's the springers' way of compensating. Even more than his daily backyard antics, this hunting season behavior is a pleasure—and a comical one at that—to behold. More than one new hunter has witnessed these athletic leaps, during which he often spins around to find us, and has broken out in laughter. I've been watching spaniels do this for twenty-five years and it still makes me laugh. My favorite part of bird hunting is watching the dogs work and, without a doubt, my favorite part of watching the dogs work is seeing these great, searching leaps. A few months ago, I managed to capture one of those leaps on camera and posted it on Facebook for my friends to see. It really was just a picture of unbridled happiness. That day, Joy coined the phrase, *be like Fred.*

We say it all the time now, especially when Fred makes us laugh out in the field, which is more frequent than you might think. There's rarely a hunt where Fred's joyfulness doesn't shine through and when he doesn't give off the impression of simple happiness to be there, and to be in the moment. Even in the shadow of his big brother's hunting prowess, Fred has developed the knack for reminding us that—while this bird hunting stuff is serious business—it also pays to have a little fun. Fred is becoming a great hunting dog, with good bird locating and retrieval instincts, but his most important attribute might just be his ability to radiate his immutable happiness.

Be like Fred.

19

SUBJECTIVE SKILL

It's hard to detect good luck. It looks so much like
something you've earned.
—*Frank A. Clark*

I LOOKED down at my hands. They were shaking. My breath came in harsh, raspy gulps. Beneath the multiple layers of clothes, carefully selected for this frigid morning, my heart pounded in a way that would likely not please my primary care physician. Fourteen feet in the air, atop an aging ladder stand, I tried to stand but my legs wobbled, and I was forced to sit back down. Thoughts jumbled in my mind. I couldn't focus. In my head, the only coherent sentence that kept forming and repeating itself was, *what on earth just happened?*

Opening day of deer season 2019 started off with a comedy of errors. Well, it would have been a comedy if things hadn't gone so wrong. Either way, it started off with a good number of errors. I was to meet Porter at a location we'd frequently hunted together. The thing was, he had put up a new stand for me in an area I wasn't familiar with. The plan was to meet before daylight so he could show me the stand. I had a rough idea, but it was so rough that I'd have no prayer of locating a camouflaged stand in the pitch blackness. The first error happened when, on their way to meet me, Porter and Melody realized that Mel had forgotten her license. They had to return home to get it, adding a good forty-minute round-trip before they'd get back to me. Porter's aggravation was evident in his tone when he called. He asked if I thought I could find the stand on my own, after giving me some detailed directions. I told him I'd try, knowing we'd be into daylight—and shooting hours—before he arrived, and he and Mel would be rushing to get into their own stand. To make a long story somewhat shorter, I was supposed to veer off on the first logging road to the left of a main trail. The stand was a few hundred yards down that trail on the right. The problem was that Porter had forgotten there were two other roads cutting off to the left before the one I'd be hunting. *Oops.* With my small but bright flashlight beaming all over the woods, I traipsed and traipsed, convincing myself that I simply hadn't seen it. So, I backtracked and circled fruitlessly. In the dark woods, I jumped several deer who crashed off into the black pre-dawn. *Damn it!* I called Porter, who said he may have forgotten about one of the trails. Hiking quickly back out to the main trail, I found the next one. More traipsing. More scaring deer off. More not finding a stand.

As the glow of twilight appeared above the hills on the eastern horizon, I began to panic. Fully dressed in insulated gear for what I assumed would be a short walk to the stand, I was now drenched in sweat. My rifle sling dug into my right shoulder, while the straps from my heavy pack dug into *both* shoulders. I knew, *knew,* I had likely ruined the area with the number of deer I scared off due to my wandering around.

Quietly steaming, both literally and figuratively, I called Porter a second time.

"You didn't find it? Uh-oh. We'll be there in a few minutes."

I'd been blindly walking around in the dark for a half-hour. When Porter's truck appeared at the edge of a dark cornfield, I walked over to meet them. Neither Porter nor Mel looked particularly happy. I'm quite sure Uncle Joel didn't look all that pleased either.

"Let's go," Porter said. "I'm surprised you didn't find it."

You and me both, kid.

As it turns out, it wasn't my orienteering skills that were lacking. We passed the first trail and Porter said, "Oh, you went down there. It's the next one." Only, it wasn't. The correct trail to the left was actually the third one. I didn't have to tease Porter. He was angry enough with himself. No need to pile on. Hurrying down what was apparently the *only* logging road I hadn't slogged down in the dark, I did my best to keep up with Porter. He was in a hurry, and it was not easy. As he slid across a patch of ice as if he were an Olympic figure skater, I carefully shuffled my heavy boots across the ice, not wanting to fall on my pack and my rifle. More than once during that fast trot down to the as-yet-unseen deer stand, I was reminded of duck hunting on that ice-covered pier with Porter and his friends almost a year ago.

Once at the stand, Porter simply said, "good luck," before departing, again at breakneck speed. I climbed the ladder stand, thankful daylight had only just begun to break in the woods. It was still early, and not quite legal shooting light. Knowing I'd be freezing from the amount of sweat generated in my woods-wandering, I stripped down my top half. It was 14°F., so it's probably not necessary to tell you that I did so *very quickly*. Removing my sweaty base-layer shirt, I stuffed it into my pack before hurriedly re-dressing myself. With the gun and pack rested on the back of my seat, relief turned to terror when I heard crunching in the woods a fair distance behind me. I looked at my watch. Legal shooting hours. Loading my old Winchester as quickly and silently as I could, I was completely unprepared if this was a shootable deer. Thankfully (well, that isn't precisely the word I should use), it was not a deer. It was another hunter, walking straight toward me. *What else can go wrong today?!* I should know better than to ask that question. Taking off my orange hat, I waved it to get his attention which, thankfully (that word, again) it did. Rather than politely wave in acknowledgement and move quietly away from the area, he yelled. Opening day. Dawn. Legal shooting light. And he *yelled.*

"Okay, okay. I *see you!*"

Oh, the thoughts I thought at that moment. I won't share them, but you can imagine. He finally stomped his way out of sight, cracking branches as he went. Maybe, just maybe, any deer in the area (ones that I hadn't already scared away into the darkness) would see him go and, once he was out of sight, think the area was safe again. I've seen the bait-and-switch tactic work in the past and tried to think hopefully that this could be the case. It was easier to think like that than to realize that not one, but *two* people had now carelessly stomped around the woods, probably driving out every last deer in the area. I was able to stay positive for about fifteen minutes. Twenty, tops. Then I just felt hopeless. In the first hour of the first day of the season, hopelessness is the exact opposite of what I wanted to feel. Porter and Mel were only four or five hundred yards from me and, sometime around 8 a.m., he let me know they had seen a handful of deer. The last text said, "Everything we've seen so far could best be described as *cute.*" That at least made me smile when smiling was the last thing I felt like doing. I put the cell phone back in my pocket and stared down at my old rifle. How many deer has that gun killed? I don't know, but it's starting to look its age. I'm going to have to replace it one of these . . .

Every last thought emptied from my mind. My head jerked up. I don't know if it was movement or sound. Months later, I don't remember what made me look up. Coming in at a fast trot, a big, mature whitetail buck was closing the distance, heading on an almost identical line as the other hunter I'd seen. His trot turned into a gallop. I still had one glove on and one off from texting with Porter. My trigger finger was thankfully (truly!) on the ungloved hand. When the distance closed to twenty-five yards, he disappeared behind a large shagbark hickory. I slid off the safety and the sound made the buck stop. He was perfectly broadside. It would have been an easy shot, even with the bow. I vaguely remember shooting him. Perhaps not. The memory is hazy, at best. One moment he was standing and the next he was down, after a short sprint into the brush behind me. The thing I distinctly remember is the sound of him hitting the ground. It was like a ton of bricks impacting the frozen oak and beech leaves, as if he had been dropped from a hundred feet up.

Although I'd had no time to panic before the shot, I quickly started to come unglued. I was shaking all over. I couldn't think straight. It's no wonder the memories are hazy because, at that moment, I was barely there. Having experienced this moment a few times, I forced myself to calm down. I was high in a tree, carrying a high-powered rifle. Despite my excitement, it was precisely the *wrong* time to get stupid. I would have been calmer if I could see the deer. All I could see was one antler peeking around yet another large oak. I waited a moment, watching for movement before lowering the rifle. I quickly reloaded and searched the ground for the buck. The startling difference in perspective when sitting in a tree and standing at the base of one is always good for a little confusion, and it took me a moment to get my bearings. As soon as I spotted the buck, panic again set in. He was alive. Only, he wasn't. His head was up. I put the scope on him and realized that he had fallen with his head wedged between two saplings. He was, thankfully (!), stone-dead.

Unloading the rifle again, I placed it under the stand and approached the buck. I've experienced the phenomenon of ground shrinkage a handful of times. This was, however, the very opposite. When I shot the deer, I had an idea that he was a good buck. I didn't pay much attention to his rack, other than to know it was pretty good. He seemed to be about the size of my last two nice 8-pointers. In body size, I thought, he may have even been smaller. I was completely incorrect. As I approached the buck, his rack seemed to grow. Freeing his head from the saplings, his head rested on its side, and his right beam towered high above his body. It took only a moment to come to the realization that I had killed the best buck of my life. Period. End of story. I looked the animal over carefully, realizing that his body was enormous. It was the size of his rack making it look smaller. Lying in the woods, he looked like a horse with antlers. Big antlers. *Once-in-a-lifetime buck.* You hear the phrase a lot if you read deer hunting magazines, but this was mine.

With shaking hands, I texted Porter.

"Big buck down," I teased, then added, "Biggest one of my life . . ."

I cannot repeat Porter's reply. It was funny, pointed, and expletive-laden. Suffice it to say, he was very happy.

I sat for a moment of quiet thanksgiving. I've shot a lot of deer. Lots and lots of deer. Sometimes I get a little choked up. Usually, I don't. I've learned to take the emotions as they come. There are good emotions, and bad emotions. They are the key ingredients that keep me returning to the deer woods for going on three decades now. Sitting on a small log next to that enormous buck, though, strong emotions flowed through me. They wracked my body. I had tears in my eyes. It wasn't the happiness of the moment, because no deer is ever going to change your life, no matter how big. It wasn't the sadness of the moment. Shooting deer doesn't make me exceptionally sad. I love to deer hunt. This time, it was the *culmination* of all those years of deer hunting. All the ups. All the downs. All the years in the woods all gathered together on this one cold November morning. And to share it with the next generation of hunters made it even more emotional. I won't try to over-analyze it for you, mostly because I can't.

Porter and Mel appeared out of nowhere shortly after. They approached the buck with reverence and a few more expletives. Porter, eyes wide with disbelief, knelt by the buck, hoisting his head off the ground, gripping his antlers and facing the great beast. Putting the head back down, he walked circles around it. He checked its teeth. He examined its hooves. He again picked up the head, turning it this time from side to side. I couldn't help smiling as Porter mirrored almost everything I did before he and Melody arrived. His reverence for the buck was palpable.

He looked at me, and I believe I saw tears in his eyes as well. I nodded. Sometimes I worry that, as successful as he's been at hunting, Porter may become jaded by that early success. This was proof to the contrary. Once Porter's inspection was over, the three of us group-hugged deep in the deer woods. Emotions flowed. It was as fine a moment as I've ever experienced deer hunting. *The* finest. Again, that feeling of *culmination* over-whelmed me. Porter put me on this deer, even though he had never seen a deer this size in these woods. He was proud of his accomplishment, as well he should have been. I just pulled the trigger on all of his hard work.

"Tell me the story," Porter said.

I told him about being depressed at having messed up the

deer woods before dawn. I told him about the other (loudmouth) hunter approaching me at dawn. I told them how a great-horned owl perched near me and hooted the early morning away. But, as for the actual shot, there wasn't much to say. *The deer ran in and I shot him.* It wouldn't make for a good magazine article. The only skill I'll credit myself with that day was being able to pull off a hasty shot. There is something to be said for hunting birds over flushing dogs. You learn to stay on your toes. That wasn't, however, what made the hunt memorable. It was the number of things that went wrong before one lucky moment caused everything to go right. That's the way with so many deer hunts I've experienced over the years. The errors, the emotions, the camaraderie, the day. These are the things that make a hunt. When that big old buck joins the others on the wall, it's not as a testament to my prowess as a hunter. It's a reminder of a day filled with emotions of all kinds. It's not just the hunt of a lifetime. It's the culmination of a lifetime of hunting.

If luck played a little part in facilitating the experience, I can accept that.

20

TO SHOOT A DOE

The place where optimism most flourishes
is the lunatic asylum.
—Havelock Ellis

THE DAY after I shot the big buck (I did mention that he was the *best buck of my life*, right?), I returned to the very same stand in the very same woods where the 9-point beast had fallen. Sunday, unlike opening Saturday twenty-four hours previous, found me surefootedly following the bouncing beam of my flashlight. I located the stand with no problem, no profusion of sweat, and no sense of stress. Things were looking up, already. Still basking in the glow of the big buck, I settled into the stand with enthusiasm. The chilled pre-dawn air was in no way detrimental to my good mood. Yesterday, it was a chilly 14°F. Today, a balmy 19°F. *Heat wave.* With two doe permits to fill in this area, and two in the state land area I also frequently hunt, I thought this day might just put another deer in the freezer. Knowing that luck seldom works that way, I have experienced enough seasons where success begat success. My most successful hunts were often parts of a larger, successful season. I certainly hoped this would be the case. While this area didn't hold large numbers of the caliber buck I took the previous morning, it held more does than anywhere I'd ever seen in my life. Following Porter's unwritten guidance about only shooting older does, and preferably those without fawns, I didn't think a big old doe would be difficult to find, even after all of the activity of yesterday's opener. As the sun bathed the woods behind me in a subtle, wintry orange glow, I searched the woods below for the big buck's gut pile. I know many hunters who will drag their deer off and field-dress them a good distance from their stands. I've never felt the need, having seen many deer step over their cousin's gut pile with little more than an indifferent sniff, if they have any reaction at all. Do they attract foxes and coyotes, vultures and hawks? Yes, sometimes. The way I see it, at least there might be a little entertainment in whatever vermin the viscera might attract. When enough light fell upon the pile, some twenty-five yards from my stand, I was unsurprised to observe most of it had already been eaten. The coyotes make short work of almost anything left very long in the western New York woods. A thin, crunchy layer of snow made my approach less than stealthy, but I settled into the big ladder stand with a fair amount of confidence—perhaps, I must admit, a bit *too* much.

A half-hour after legal daylight, movement to the north caught my eye and my hand tightened involuntarily on the stock of my rifle. It was the same trail on which the big buck approached just twenty-three hours earlier. Yesterday I didn't have the luxury of advanced notice. Today, I was paying attention. As a deer materialized a hundred and twenty yards out through the mixed hardwoods, I couldn't tell what it was. All I could tell was that it was a good-sized deer. With the naked eye, it appeared to be a big doe. Since it was headed in my direction, there was no sense making a hasty decision. When it rounded a small downed oak top, the deer suddenly lowered and raised its head in rhythmic, familiar motions. It was making a rub which meant, of course, this was not a doe. Reaching carefully for the binoculars hanging from the stand behind me, I took my eyes off the buck for a few moments. It's always amazing how a large deer can blend in and disappear so seamlessly into the relatively open woods. When I did locate him, I realized he had disappeared behind yet another top. Peeking out from behind it, his eyes were locked on mine, or at least on my binoculars. He'd seen me move before I saw him. The buck, now less than a hundred yards out, was far larger than I had initially thought. Had this been twenty-three hours earlier, I would have been more than happy to shoot this deer. Likely only about half the size of the one I *did* shoot, I would have gladly taken him and, I'm quite sure, been very proud of that fact. Mature bucks don't grow on trees and this was, without a doubt, a mature buck. While the big 9-pointer had whitish, sweeping high antlers, this somewhat smaller 8-pointer had a more traditional symmetrical rack, and was burnished dark, likely from rubbing on the plentiful conifers in the area. He was a beautiful buck. I didn't want to spook him, but was tired of the eye strain of watching him through the binoculars, as well as the effort it took to hold them up. I slowly lowered them, reaching around behind me to hang them back on the stand. I thought the motion might scare the buck off, but it had no effect. We watched each other a moment longer, and the buck resumed feeding, heading steadily in my direction. Passing the gut pile at twenty yards, he didn't pay any attention to it. Passing *me* at twenty-five, he did cast two glances up at me to let me know he knew I was there, but he didn't seem phased by my presence.

If he'd experienced any hunting pressure in the last few days, it hadn't had an adverse effect on him. Perhaps sensing he had given me too much credit, he made a wide arc around me, passing broadside most of the way. At no point was he any more than sixty yards from me. He didn't seem to be in a hurry. I had an idea. Glancing around to ensure I wasn't missing any opportunities to fill my doe tag, I reached into my coat pocket very carefully and extracted my cell phone. Fiddling with the camera, which I rarely use, I quickly turned on the video function and filmed the very calm, mature whitetail buck passing within rifle range. The stand was located at the base of a small finger of woods jutting out into a large cut cornfield and the buck was obviously making a beeline for the corn. That he was going *to* it rather than coming in *from* it made me wonder if this deer had any clue that deer season was under way. If the big buck's actions yesterday were any indication, the memo may not have made it to this part of the deer woods quite yet. The 8-pointer passed through the small ribbon of heavy cover and out into the corn, where he vacuumed up loose kernels about forty yards from me. Far more exposed on the field side, I found myself holding my breath. Startling me yet again, the big buck closed the distance, turning and walking up the edge of the field. Now only fifteen yards from me, he lifted his nose several times in my direction. I was sure he was going to bolt out of there. He didn't but, rather, returned to eating. Once again, I sneaked my phone out of my jacket and took a few still photos as he gulped corn only twenty yards from me.

Well, this is weird.

On some cue, he walked off across the enormous field. There was another hunter's ground-blind several hundred yards out into the field and I found myself waiting for the shot. No one was in it, I supposed, when the buck passed within fifty yards and no shot rang out. Maybe someone *was* in it, but they have higher standards than I. I don't know, though. Their standards would be ridiculously high not to shoot that buck. He was a beauty. It didn't dawn on me until later that night there may well have been another hunter in that stand, but he, too, had already filled his buck tag and was relegated to doe hunting. You never know. In the evening, I did a short still-hunt along the edge of yet another giant cornfield and came upon another, smaller 8-pointer along with what looked to be a decent 6-point buck. After years of not seeing *too* many bucks, my life was suddenly full of them.

I didn't see a single doe. Not one.

Porter wanted to get Melody a crack at her first buck and, when we met after dark, after showing them the video of the first buck, I told them the exact location on the cornfield where I saw the other two. I suggested they set up there at daylight. I'd move farther down the field, where I found a heavily tracked-up area near the river bottom which I hoped would be the ticket to filling one of my doe tags. It seemed like a good plan.

They all *seem* like good plans.

Daylight found us creeping along the edge of the same cornfield along which I'd crept the night before. I dropped Porter and Mel in a low spot, near the end of an irrigation boom, where I'd seen the bucks. I quickly covered another five or six hundred yards, where a small spigot of woods stuck out in the field and in which I was pleased to see several deeply rutted deer trails coming up and out of the river bottom. A few acres of corn still stood here, with a thin strip cut between the woods and the remaining corn. *Perfect*. Trying hard to not overthink it, I settled in just inside the brush at the edge of the cornfield, halfway between two of the big deer trails. If they came out of the river bottom, I'd have a snap shot at them before they disappeared across the cut strip and into the sea of standing cornstalks beyond.

It was another cold morning. A very cold morning in deer country is a thing of beauty, once you realize that you've dressed correctly, despite the sweat running down your neck from the long walk. I settled in, but I felt . . . twitchy. Unlike the place I'd left my hunting partners where they'd have a hundred-yard shot in a couple of directions should any deer appear, my own shooting would have to be fast. There wouldn't be much room for error and, I knew, any deer that popped into the small opening were likely to realize I was there at the same time I realized *they* were there. Perhaps still a bit cocky at my hasty shot at the big buck two days earlier, I kept telling myself *you can do it. Just relax.* Relaxed isn't my default mode, especially when deer hunting, so I had to settle for *twitchy.* It wasn't easy to remain perfectly motionless, but I gave it my best. Inwardly I was twitching like a jumping bean.

The sun was up for an hour or more when I heard motion in the brush behind me, by the side of the river. The steady *whoosh-whoosh-whoosh* told me it was a deer, if not more than one. Trying to steady my (*twitchy*) ragged breathing, I quietly opened the scope covers, made sure it was dialed down to its lowest magnification, and waited. At one point, the deer sounded like it passed only five or six yards behind me. My (*twitchy*) nerves jangled. There was no remedy for such excitement, other than to ride it out. The deer paused in the brush for around five minutes. In retrospect, it may have been five seconds, but time seemed to drag on interminably while I waited. As if sensing the coast was clear, it moved forward toward the thin strip of cut corn, its large chestnut body becoming visible through the thinning screen of brush. Before it fully made it into the clearing, I could see the antlers.

Another buck. Never in my hunting career had I been more disappointed to see a buck. While not a *mature* buck, it was still a nice buck. Again, if it had been a couple of days ago, I probably would have shot it. The deer, much smaller in body than yesterday's 8-pointer, stepped into the clearing. It bore the thin neck of a younger deer. Probably a 2-year-old buck. I tried to disappear back into the brush, while my boots stuck out into the thin, open strip. Once again, figuring I had little to lose, I fished my phone out of my coat and began shooting video. The buck emerged fifteen yards from me. The steam from his nose made symmetrical clouds in the cold, morning air. Rather than dash across the opening and into the corn, as an older, wiser buck may have done, he fed. For a few moments, he moved slowly, steadily in my direction. With no wind, he hadn't scented me. Camouflage and all, however, it wasn't like I was invisible. When the buck closed the distance to five yards, I had to resist the urge to lean forward and poke him. It's rare during gun season to be that close to a buck, or any deer, for that matter. I was at once thrilled and mystified. I couldn't believe the deer didn't see me yet. We shared the same space, his cloud of breath mixing with my own. These moments bring me back to whitetail country year after year. Perhaps he finally winded me or simply sensed something was wrong about that shape in the low brush next to the cornfield. Either way, he turned and stepped quickly into the corn, where he again slowed and started feeding, still within fifteen yards of me. When he finally vanished into the corn maze, I realized he was headed for Porter and Mel. I sent them a text and let them know he might pop out in their location.

Of course, he never did.

Tuesday morning, day four of gun season, found me again in the ladder stand where my big buck fell. There had to be a doe or two there. Fresh deer sign plastered the area, obvious after a light, overnight snowfall. Daylight broke on slightly warmer temperatures, probably a result of the low cloud cover from the passing front. I didn't mind spending *one* morning in the relative comfort of 30°F. temperatures. It was still cold enough for deer to be on the move and besides, I told myself, sometimes the *best* deer movement is after a passing front. Dutifully scanning the woods and limiting my motion, I hunted as diligently as I had every day since legal daylight dawned on opening day. This would be a short hunt, as I had some obligations to tend to in the afternoon, but I would hunt just as hard, still hoping to get a doe or two to agree to spending the next few months in our freezer.

When 11 a.m. rolled around, I'd seen nothing more to keep my interest than a pair of fat fox squirrels running off a comparatively small gray, and a pair of tom turkeys feeding in the adjacent cornfield. Each was good for two minutes of entertainment in the otherwise boring four hours. As I scanned the woods one last time before climbing down, movement in the corn to the right caught my eye. I assumed, incorrectly, the turkeys had returned. An enormous 8-pointer stepped from the thick brush behind me and into the corn. He didn't feed, and he didn't linger, as the other (dumber) 8 had. He moved purposefully across the field, passing me broadside at about forty-five yards. He was the fourth buck I could have taken with a chip-shot in four days. I shook my head, barely believing it. I trained the binoculars on him. His dark, chocolate rack stood high above his head. When he turned his head at the sound of a distant, passing truck, I could see he was every bit as wide as the monster I'd shot on opening day. As I waited for him to disappear into the far thicket so I could climb down without spooking him, I said an informal prayer, asking God if he might see fit to spread a couple of these bucks out over the next few years rather than dump them all in my lap during the first few days of the 2019 season. It was starting to get depressing.

How hard can it be to shoot a doe?

21

IT WASN'T ALWAYS LIKE THIS

Youth cannot know how age thinks and feels. But old men
are guilty if they forget what it was to be young.
—J.K. Rowling

WATCHING PORTER drag the fat doe uphill on uneven ground, I felt—not for the first time—old. While he didn't appear to struggle under a hundred-odd pounds of very fresh venison trailing behind him, I was tasked only with carrying our coats and rifles. It should have been me, since I had shot the deer. Probably not wanting to witness me struggling, Porter simply grabbed the drag harness, and off he went. Barely slowing down, he crossed a small brook, full of water. Reaching the brook, already a minute behind Porter, I stepped in, nearly losing my balance and all of our gear, before righting myself. By the time I pulled myself up the opposite bank, Porter and the doe were resting near the edge of a grass field. Finally catching up with him, only because he'd stopped moving, I tried to hide my breathlessness. That, of course, didn't go well and I erupted into a ragged cough. Porter studiously ignored my gyrations. He's a good hunting partner. Inwardly, I thought *I am in pretty good shape!* Of course, trailing on that thought was another unwelcomed inner voice that continued, *for your age.*

It wasn't always like this.

There was a time, not that long ago, when I was the youngest guy in a group of varyingly older guys. Wait, I should fix that. It was, in fact, *that long ago.* Doing the math on past experiences these days is always an exercise in surprise. Some of those early hunts were when I was, like Porter, in my early 20s. Deer hunting with a bunch of guys who ranged in age from their early 30s to their late 70s, I was frequently recruited for the dirty work and the hard labor. And, I must admit, I loved it. When one of the older guys in our group dropped a deer, I was often asked to drag it out. Sometimes, I was even asked to do the field-dressing. As I recall, I didn't mind, since I needed all the practice I could get back then. Trust me, by my third or fourth deer season, I was well experienced in field-dressing, dragging, and hanging deer. Often cheered on and instructed by the older hunters, I took pride in my assignments and executed them with an enthusiasm that I still feel today, though with less energy to actuate such endeavors. I think the older hunters probably watched me with the same thoughts that I now watched Porter: *Oh, thank God he's here to drag it for me!*

One late morning in the very late eighties, I was high on a hilltop in the Catskill Mountains. Two of my hunting partners were my future kids' great-grandfathers. They were instrumental in showing me the hunting ropes, since I did not start hunting until I was 20. I'd learned a lot by listening to their advice. I returned the favor by always taking care of their deer for them. The season had been a poor one, and we'd discussed the previous night about putting on a deer drive high on the hill where the deer had not yet been bothered. It was a good plan. In those days, the Catskills were still teeming with deer and it was an unpleasant surprise to have such an unproductive season. The *drive* simply consisted of me walking through a thick bedding area and then down a long ravine where the two great-grandfathers waited by an old barbed-wire fence. The hilltop had once been a cow pasture, and the remnant stone walls and occasional stretches of wire had not yet completely fallen to the ensuing sixty years. As I entered the beech thicket, white tails bounced out ahead of me and, thankfully, in the right direction. One large doe broke off from the group and doubled back around, passing within twenty yards of me. I shot her without even thinking. One moment she was running and the next, my old Winchester Model 94 lever-action roared and she was down. Quickly glancing around for landmarks, I found a huge, ancient hemlock tree and quickly dragged the doe a few yards to its base, where I'd easily find her later. They were big woods and losing her was a distinct possibility. Continuing out of the thicket, I turned left into the ravine and, before I had gone a dozen feet, two shots rang out, one right after the other. That's not usually a good sign. Hustling down the ravine to see what happened, I could still see deer tails bobbing off in the distance, well past my standers' ambush.

I spotted the two hunters, each of them up on their feet and about a hundred yards apart. As I neared, I could see Lyn, clad in all black and red Woolrich plaid, kneeling by a large doe. I shook his hand, because that's what you do, but left him quickly to see what else had transpired. Howard Sr. also had a deer down, a small 6-point buck. Three deer in five minutes! That's the way you put a positive spin on a negative season!

I told Howard that I would take care of his buck. Together, we backtracked to Lyn. I also offered to gut and drag his deer out. *Youth*. Lyn had a bad time getting up the hill to start with, so I suggested that he and Howard head down together, for safety's sake, and I'd bring the deer down. They agreed. I'd like to say they *reluctantly agreed,* but if my memory serves correctly, that was not the case.

Sometime around noon, I started on the buck. Quickly field-dressing him, his spindly antlers made a convenient drag handle. In addition to the hill from the road, there was a steep ravine that needed to be crossed. I completed that with what could not honestly be described as *ease* as I struggled with the buck. It seemed a little bigger now, after a few hundred yards of hillside. At a big meadow near the top of the hill and overlooking the road, I put the buck up against another ancient stone wall for safekeeping. Retreating to Lyn's doe, I gutted that quickly, electing a different route through the big woods. I took a path that, while it avoided the steepest part of the ravine, added perhaps another five hundred yards of dragging. It took some time. The steep hill down to the road aided in the drag. I hustled the buck down to the road, and then the doe, each trip back up the steep hill slowing me just a bit more. It was grueling work. Once the two deer were down, the old men helped me load them in their trucks.

"Are you okay to get yours out of there?" Howard Sr. asked.

"No problem." Fifty-two-year-old Joel laughs heartily at that memory. *Haha!*

"You probably shouldn't wait too long. Coyotes."

He wasn't wrong.

The great-grandfathers' trucks disappeared down the twisting road, and I was left alone with the prospect of climbing that hill once again, scaling the ravine, gutting my doe, rinse, and repeat. Even at 21 years old, the thought was daunting. Born in the flatlands, I was not a natural mountain goat. Still, *coyotes.* I thought about getting a few gulps of water at the springhouse before making my third and final recovery, but the springhouse was *farther* downhill. I had no desire to engage in any more elevation changes than those that already lay ahead of me.

It took a moment or twenty of wandering to find the stately hemlock. The old doe had already started to stiffen up. I got immediately to work on her. Once ready to go, I had to give an extra tug to get her out of the small depression in which I'd hidden her. I felt a twinge in my back that these days is just a natural part of getting out of bed in the morning. Back then it was new and strange. If only I'd known! I didn't pause at the hilltop this time, rather hurrying down to the truck. There was no one around to help me get her up on the high tailgate of my own truck. I hadn't thought about that. It took some effort. Once the big doe was loaded, I walked slowly down to the springhouse to gulp what I remember as gallons and gallons of icy water. Looking back uphill toward my truck, I suddenly didn't have an ounce of energy left to get back up there. I laid down in the snow next to the springhouse and looked up to the sky, tired, but satisfied with the day. I only stayed in that position for ten minutes or so before I rebounded enough to get back to the truck. Fairly well exhausted, I wondered if it would be worth going back uphill and having a sit for the rest of the afternoon. I still had a buck tag to fill.

Those were the days.

At the truck, I helped Porter lift the big, old doe onto the tailgate. He barely seemed to have broken a sweat. I asked how he was doing. He said, not surprisingly, "We still have some daylight left . . . I have an idea."

I remember being that guy.

22

SILLY

LOOKING THROUGH my older hunting notes, I came across this day from exactly ten years ago. A lifetime ago, now. John has been retired to Florida for years. My girls were still both teenagers. Porter would have been 15. I was in my early 40s, thinking that I was getting on in years . . .

The first thing that struck me about the neatly typed notes was the word *silly*. It was typed just like this: *SILLY!* And it was pretty silly. Sitting in John's stand, I was having anything but a wonderful wilderness experience. From the tree stand, I could see his neighbor's house, his house, his tractor, his car, and my truck parked in his driveway. The stand was erected, according to John, as a result of seeing a few deer recently in his small orchard. It was more of a fallback place if he had only a short time to hunt, and I don't think he ever hunted it. Now I saw why. Looking over at his house, and practically into his front living room window, it just seemed silly. *Silly!*

Prior to the start of gun season, a long, slow bow season culminated in my arrowing a single, small doe. I had high hopes, due to the amount of rutting sign around my stands, that gun season would prove more productive. It didn't. 2010 was just one of those years. I've had a few. I hunted hard during bow season, and hunted even harder during gun season, and it just wasn't meant to be. At this point, late in the month of November, a little silliness was warranted, I suppose. Maybe it was even required. I settled into the tree stand, pulled my hat down against the bitter cold, and waited. Still, the feeling of absurdity gnawed at my cold bones. *Silly* eventually went away and I started thinking, this is *stupid*.

The season hadn't started this way. On opening morning, weeks prior, everything was very serious. I headed out of the house well before daylight and hiked to a tree stand in a heavy deer-traffic area. There was a scrape not twenty yards from the stand I'd selected. It had been freshened every day of the last few days of bow season, though I'd yet to see the buck that was doing the work. Based on the size of some nearby rubs, I knew that a monster was in the area although, during bow season, I had only seen one smaller buck. When I climbed into the stand before daylight on opening day, I had vivid premonitions of getting my crosshairs on the big buck. As slow as archery season had been, however, I'm sure I would have taken the smaller buck. Sunrise came quickly, as it always does on a clear day in the flatlands. Squirrels shuffled through the leaves below me and a gray fox briefly appeared in the distance, probably on his way back to bed for the day. Everything seemed positive. Around 8 a.m. I poured myself a small lid full of coffee from my Thermos and scanned the woods. The lethargy of hours and days on stand hadn't arrived yet. It was opening day. Deer season was new again. I was ready for something to happen at any moment. It did. As I finished the last few drops of coffee, I heard something to the right and behind me. Quietly spinning the Thermos lid back on, I dropped it into the pack hanging next to me and grabbed my muzzleloader off its hanger. Craning my neck around as far as possible, I couldn't discern the source of the noise. Though the impenetrable thicket was less dense than it had been during archery season, it still was capable of hiding a big deer—even one that was relatively close. Standing as carefully and quietly as I could, I turned toward the source of the noise and immediately spotted it. Antlers moved from east to west through the brush. And that was *all* I could see. It was as if someone was carrying deer antlers on the end of a tall pole. The buck itself was nowhere in sight, but the upper part of its rack was clear as day. It didn't take more than a glance to realize this was a monster. His rack carried at least ten long points, maybe more. I didn't stop to count but knew this was the monster who made the big rubs and scrapes around the stand. At only fifty or sixty yards out, it shouldn't be a hard shot. Hunting with the muzzleloader by choice, though, I knew I had to wait for a better-than-average shot. One deflection would mean a lost deer. The buck moved steadily but quickly through the thicket. Bracing the muzzleloader against the tree trunk, I scanned over the scope, looking out ahead of the buck's travel route and trying to anticipate the shot. A small opening was coming, just ten yards ahead of the buck. I trained the scope on it and held my breath. As the buck reached a small willow tree to the right of the shooting lane, I lowered my head to the scope and pulled back the hammer. Knowing better, I pictured him hanging on the wall. Only a few seconds passed but it was too long. Lifting my head, I searched for the deer, panicking. Leaning out over the tree stand, I looked around the willow tree, and could see the buck's fat rear end disappearing in the distance. Before I could lean out far enough to get the cross-hairs on him in hopes he might turn again, he disappeared.

It happened that fast.

Fast forward to late season. The setting: high above the forest floor, practically in my hunting partner's side yard. Watching John, clad in orange, disappear out his driveway, head down the road, and slip into the woods a few hundred yards away, I didn't feel silly or even stupid any longer. I just felt *ridiculous*. But, after the letdown of the season it had been, a little *ridiculousness* might just be in order. Over the years, we've pushed the narrow little thicket next to his house dozens of times. While we've pushed deer out of it, no one ever got one. They seem to know that no one would shoot in the direction of the house and have escaped out through the yard several times. To the east lie vast thickets, cornfields, and open shooting. They rarely go that way, of course.

John had only been out of sight perhaps three minutes when I heard crashing and branches breaking. Naturally, I assumed it was him. The little one-man push doesn't take more than a few minutes. When the first doe materialized on the trail, running full out, I was completely caught off-guard. I got my handgun up only quickly enough to see her disappear across the opening. She was in my shooting lane for no more than a second. I was kicking myself for daydreaming when the second doe came, also running as if she was on fire. With my revolver still up in the shooting position from the first encounter, my heart pounded as the second doe crossed the same opening and the red dot on my scope found her chest. She dropped only twenty yards from me. I could barely believe it. Any feelings of silliness began to fade, as I realized I pulled off one of my best handgun shots ever. Suddenly, the season didn't seem so dismal, the day not quite as silly. Just then, John's wife Carmine came out the front door of their house, a steaming cup of coffee in her hand. She approached the downed deer, looking up at me, still in the stand, and saying, "You got one! I heard you shoot!"

It was just so silly.

23

DEER CAMP

I'VE BEEN doing this for a long time.

I have deer hunted much longer than some of my hunting partners, though I'm by no means an old-timer. Just ask me. I have friends who have been at this decades longer than I have. I've never claimed to be an *expert*. Deer hunting is too much fun and I don't want to ruin it with the pressure of having to exhibit *expertise*. I do, however, think I've earned the rank of *veteran* at least. I've been chasing deer for the better part of thirty years, so this is not a new experience for me. Don't call me jaded, though. I'm not. Since that first hunt in 1987 there is not much in life that excites me like the night before the opening day of gun season for whitetail deer. During these thirty-odd years, that has not changed one bit. The excitement is there, ever-present. Maybe even more present in the past few years. Hitting the mid-century mark makes you appreciate the gift of time and its fleeting nature. I acknowledge the passing of time more than ever these days. There's no hanging on and wishing it wasn't happening. There is only embracing the days you have and making the most of each of them. I work on that every day.

Deer season brings home the passage of time to me more than any other time of the year. There is never a year that passes in the deer woods without poignant lessons about life, loss, and those teachings only time in nature can reveal. Learning is the best way to make the most of our time and I still learn something new every October and November. Sometimes those lessons are simply what *not* to do next time but, more often than not, there is true learning to be had.

Part of deer season is deer camp. It is and always has been a very big part. I am afraid that the traditions surrounding deer camp are rapidly fading in the face of the modernization of hunting and the solitude that seems to go hand in hand with the new truths of hunting in the modern day. Everything now seems hyper-focused on tactics and techniques, technology and equipment, success and numbers. I fear the traditional things such as *fun* and *sharing* and, most important, *camaraderie*, are falling by the wayside in favor of high success rates, pressure, and competition. It's too easy to forget what's important, for people of any age.

The solitary aspect of deer hunting always meant archery season for me, more than during any other part of hunting season. Bow hunting is, almost by necessity, a sport for loners. The finesse and techniques involved are very personal and for the most part don't lend themselves well to a team effort. Back when archery hunting deer was my number one passion, phone calls were made between my small group of friends after arriving home from the deer stand. Information was passed and stories were told. It was deer camp via landline. Later on, with the advent of cell phones, we could pass information and hunting tales via text, almost in real time. Back then, texting was a new and wonderful luxury. I'm afraid now, though, that easy communication has made it far *too* easy to not have to really spend time talking with each other, much as it has in our everyday lives. What fun is that? It's a whole new, different world with this wonderful technology—technology that I fully embrace and use to its maximum potential—but it also robs us of that genuine face-to-face or at least voice-to-voice camaraderie. It's an excuse not to need an excuse and that's a shame. Sometimes new and different doesn't necessarily mean new and *better*.

Deer Camp 2018 was not deer camp via cell phone. It was, in fact, a more traditional deer camp than I have ever experienced. After spending the last few years in loner mode, hunting a quiet, backwoods ravine on public land during opening weekend, I accepted a long-offered invitation to hunt at a camp belonging to Norm, a friend of my brother-in-law. Norm's camp is a cabin tucked away in the steep hillsides of southwestern New York's Allegany County. The cabin itself *looks* like a deer camp, with rustic wooden siding, nestled into the woods on three sides, with the fourth side looking out over a vast, open expanse of the rounded, ancient Allegany Mountains and farmland. Everything about the scenery says *deer country* and everything about the cabin appearance says *deer camp*. Inside are all the comforts and accoutrements of a modern deer camp. A big fireplace surrounded by racks to hang hunting clothes keeps the cabin toasty against the cold November and December temperatures. A bedroom with multiple bunks serves as our sleeping quarters. There are hot showers and a bathroom that doesn't induce frostbite in your nether regions. A fully outfitted kitchen, complete with *coffee,* offers all the luxuries of home. It's hard to imagine needing anything more from deer camp than what Norm's camp has to offer.

Deer camp isn't always like this.

Over the course of these many years pursuing white tail deer,

deer camp has been many different things. My earliest deer camp was my own home in the Catskill Mountains. I'd make the twenty-minute drive to a large swath of private land where a small group of friends and family had exclusive access to hundreds of acres of prime deer country. Camp, in those days, meant having morning coffee at the tailgate of someone's truck. At lunch, we ate liverwurst sandwiches and drank more coffee off the same tailgate. At night, we went home, often with one or more deer. Those early days were good, and I never felt that our version of deer camp was lacking. Other years, as time and people—myself included—moved on, deer camp was some-times in the basement of a family member or friend. For several of the last years that we hunted the Catskills, deer camp was a cheap motel and a variety of greasy diners. The motel was just a place to tell our day's stories, share some laughs, and sleep. It was no less a deer camp than any other deer camp I've been a part of. A few years back, deer camp was meeting Porter at a small parking area in the Adirondack Mountains, hundreds of miles from home, in the pouring rain for an early-season muzzleloader hunt. The meeting was grim, yet purposeful, as we pulled our clothes on in the pre-dawn gloom and tried to stay dry before venturing up a steep oak ridge where we'd most certainly be getting wet. I won't soon forget the late-day, muted *boom* of Porter's muzzleloader. As we loaded his first Adirondack deer—a fine doe—into his truck, the tailgate once again became our makeshift deer camp. We were wet, tired, and sore from the steep climb (well, I was anyway . . .), but the festive meeting and handshake and photos at the end of the day was as wonderful a moment as I've had at more traditional deer camps.

The last few seasons, before accepting the invitation to Norm's camp, deer camp was yet again . . . different. Each morning during the opening weekend of the season and on into the following week, I'd leave my home at 4 a.m. and drive one hour to a large patch of public land in the hills of Wyoming County, New York. Hunting with my dogs during bird season, I'd discovered a distant ravine with some brushy draws that were heavy with deer sign. My hunches proved correct and the ravine, over the course of a few years, provided several big deer and venison for the freezer. Though accompanied by friends on a few occasions, my deer camp during those few years was mostly a lonely affair. Though I enjoy the solitude inherent in deep-woods hunting, I missed the camaraderie of years past, truth be told. No quiet jokes at the tailgate. No second-guessing how much to wear and not to wear. No complaining about the early hour combined with the lack of coffee. During those hunts, as much as I appreciate the allure of an uninterrupted day in the woods, I relied on my cell phone to keep tabs on my friends and have at least a small bit of human interaction which can, at times, flavor the bland quiet of a deerless day. Reports came in from my nephew in the Finger Lakes, John in Kentucky, Keith only a few miles away, Steve in the Allegany Mountains. We all kept each other apprised of the current state-of-the-deer season. Cell reception was lacking in my area but, every now and then, a quiet vibration deep in my jacket signaled one of my far-flung hunting partners had taken a deer or witnessed an interesting sight. I welcomed those buzzes. On day five of my lonely last hunting season, I resolved to join up with the others at Norm's camp for the final weekend of the season. It had been a quiet, unproductive week, other than a large doe taken on opening day, and a real deer camp sounded good right about then. The year ended with a last-day, last-minute 7-point buck. Celebrating with friends and family deep in the dark woods as we brought the deer out made me re-think my recent years of solitude. Though it isn't a pre-requisite for deer camp, there is a lot to be said for good company.

This year, I found myself at Norm's camp on opening weekend, breaking my own recent public land tradition in favor of
exploring a new one. My brother-in-law Steve, nephew Eric,
Norm, and Norm's nephew Michael all piled into the cabin the
Friday night before opening day. Once gear was stowed, beds
were made, and the clothes were laid out for the coming morning, talk turned to hunting as I'm sure it does every opening day
eve all over deer country. Locations were discussed. Weather
and wind direction were hot topics on a cold night. Equipment
was checked and re-checked and passed around for the others
to admire. The young guys boasted about things about which
they had no right to boast, while the old guys complained about
our aches and pains. Talk turned to deer and who would shoot
the first 12-pointer. Jabs and barbs were traded along with stories of other years' dramatic successes and comical failures. It
was deer camp during deer season in deer country and there
was no place I'd rather be.

Reflections

Whitetail buck checking the wind.

Mature whitetail buck on alert.

The author and his 2019 9-point buck.

Sunrise in the beech woods.

Porter, dragging a whitetail doe.

Porter and Joel with a late-season double.

Early season whitetail doe.

Whitetail doe in full winter coat.

Young hunters on a frigid, late-season duck hunt.

Long-tailed duck on Lake Ontario.

Rooster pheasant in flight, late season.

Max, with a limit of October roosters.

Joel, Max, and Porter with three roosters.

Fred, in full flight.

Max, showing how a pretty retrieve is done.

24

CURRENT EVENTS, 2019

ONE OF the blessings of writing about the things you're passionate about is that the documentation of those passions is always around to be remembered. It can be a curse, as well. Reading through things I wrote thirty years ago can be a painful lesson on how *not* to write and, in some cases, how not to *be*. Before embarking on a new book, I usually sit down and read my old ones. I use the writing successes as a template for what works, and the less engaging writing as a warning about what *doesn't*. I think it's an unofficial rule that you aren't supposed to admit that you read your own writing, but I also think that most writers do. The ones *I* know do, anyway. I'm not too cool. I read my old writings. It's a good window to the past and, since my writing comes mostly straight from the heart, it's a good reminder of the person I used to be. Good reminder? Well, it's a reminder, anyway.

A few weeks back I posted a comment on Facebook about a deer hunting story (someone else's) in *Deer & Deer Hunting* magazine and the next day I had a private message from a guy named Roger.

"Are you the same Joel Spring that wrote an article called *Current Events*?" He was asking, he said, because the article stuck with him and was one of the inspirations for him to take up writing, as well.

I wracked my brain. I was certain I *had* written an article called *Current Events*, but the memory was foggy, at best. I've been a pretty good steward of the Joel Spring writing collection over the years because, let's face it, who else is going to do it? In the back of my bedroom closet, nestled snugly between my gun safes, stands a book rack brimming with almost every magazine article I've written. I lost two or three over the years by lending them out but, for the most part, the museum is complete. At the top left of the stacks are my oldest articles, while at the bottom right the newest entries reside. On a whim, I started with the oldest stack and, just a few issues down, found the issue of *Deer & Deer Hunting* that contained *Current Events*. I didn't pay much attention to the magazine itself, just happy that I was able to locate it. I took a photo of the article and sent it to Roger. His response surprised me.

"It's twenty-five years old! 1994!"

I hadn't paid attention to the date, but it was, indeed, 1994. Letting Roger know that I found two copies, I asked him if he'd like the extra, since it meant something to him. He did. We've been in touch ever since and he has, in turn, shared his wonderfully inspired writing with me. Roger Page. Look him up. As I mentioned at the beginning of this chapter, having your words, memories, and thoughts right there in black and white can be both a blessing and a curse. A week passed before I picked up the magazine and forced myself to read what 25-year-old Joel Spring had to say. I'd be lying if I didn't say I was a bit afraid. 1994 was a long time ago. I was the father of two very young daughters. One of those kids' lifetimes spanned the years between 1993 and 2016, when I lost

Jennifer to brain cancer at 23. To say 1994 was a lifetime ago would not be at all inaccurate. Not only *my* world, but *the* world was different back then. The news of the day that seemed so important then ended up being mostly forgotten footnotes. Probably the most notorious event, for Americans anyway, was OJ Simpson being charged in two deaths. The slow-speed white Bronco chase was riveting to a bored populace. Nancy Kerrigan got kneecapped by an associate of her Olympic rival. Kurt Cobain killed himself. Record of the Year was "I Will Always Love You," by Whitney Houston. *ER* and *Friends* debuted, starting their iconic runs as wildly successful television shows. It all seems so silly now.

Taking a deep breath, a week after my latest exchange with Roger Page, I began reading *Current Events, 1994*, curious about what young Joel had to say.

Current Events

After scanning the barrage of bad news and broken political promises on the newspaper's front page, I turned—as I do every day—to the "letters" section. It's always more interesting to see what the average person thinks about current events than what some overworked and not particularly interested writer has digested and regurgitated from the news wire.

One guy, a World War II vet, denounced the Clinton administration for his policy on gays in the military. The next letter applauded the president for his open-mindedness. I tried to picture the two letter writers seated across from each other, arguing it out over a couple of beers. Good for a chuckle.

I skipped down through the drudgery of local politics and scanned for something far more interesting. Every once in a while, a letter writer tackled deer management problems. A township nearby hadn't allowed hunting for several years and now was suffering the Housing Development vs. Unchecked

Deer Herd syndrome. Someone proposed a limited hunting season, and self-proclaimed "environmentalists" came howling out of their condo's artificial woodwork.

Buried within this letter were phrases like "Horrors of hunting," "Gun-toting Rambos," and "Horrible Suffering," and all of the usual uninformed emotionalism that comes with discussions of animal population control. The letter was written by a typical anti-hunting "animal lover" who was no doubt convinced that The Discovery Channel had made her an expert in all things wildlife management. So it goes.

I reached for my pen and notebook and began to compose a letter of my own. I've tried, fairly regularly, to counter each false representation of hunting with a reasonable, thoughtful hunter's point of view. The editor has been fair and published each of them. About halfway through this letter, though, I gave up. What I was saying had been said, by me and others, hundreds of times in that same space. Sure, her letter was full of misinformation (yes, I'd like to call them lies, but won't) and preconceived notions about hunters and hunting, but what's the use? The people reading these letters have brains. They have the ability to distinguish scientific information from emotional drivel. I put my pen down, ripped the three-by-five sheet from my notebook, and tossed it into the kitchen trash. Two points. The public was on its own with this one.

I tried to forget the ridiculous letter and moved on through the rest of the paper. On the next page was a follow-up to the trial of the two boys accused of kidnapping a toddler from an English shopping mall and brutally killing him. Incredible. Two little kids committing murder. Do you want to talk horror?

On the next page was an in-depth look at an Illinois family that lost everything to the Mississippi River. Family farmhouse and outbuildings, handed down through five generations, all gone. Washed away in the flood. Do you want to tell me about the fragility of nature? It doesn't seem so fragile right now, does it.

A boy of fifteen was apprehended when trying to sell crack cocaine to undercover officers from his ten-speed bike. Would you like to tell me how we have to worry less about people and more about wildlife? I'm far more worried about raising a generation of children with lost souls, with no rich traditions to look back on, and even less to look forward to. Yeah, the kids can take care of themselves. It's the poor deer we should worry about, right?

Come on.

Let's see, here's the story about the Bosnian family that was burned to death by flame throwers. And the boatload of refugees that capsized, killing all aboard while waiting for a glimpse of the freedoms we so badly abuse. Then there's the small-town cop who was ambushed and shot three times at point-blank range, and another officer killed in a car crash while rushing to his aid. He left a wife and three boys, ages two, four, and six. That's not supposed to happen to the good guys, right? That crash was four miles from my house. Do you still want to talk about suffering? I think I've had enough for one day.

When I go into the woods to hunt deer, I don't go to cause pain or suffering. There's an excess of that in the "civilized" world. I don't go to commit "unspeakable horrors."

I go to escape them.

—End—

Editor's note—The writing was painful to re-read and, in re-typing the article for this book, I must admit I wanted to do some serious editing. That writing was my writing in 1994, so I left it untouched. To fairly review the article,

I'll say that I did like it, almost to my surprise and most definitely to my relief. Young Joel was more opinionated, perhaps more close-minded, but he was what I'd ultimately become.

To the news stories in the articles, many of them hit home now that a quarter of a century has passed. The deer herds in the rapidly sprawling Buffalo suburbs had to finally be reduced by police snipers. Hunting would never again happen in that area. What was the conclusion? The suburb is still overrun with deer and would benefit greatly from a controlled hunt. I think we all know now, though, that ship has sailed. About the anti-hunting letter writer? I would never call her a typical anti-hunter now. I've learned that no one—hunter, non-hunter, anti-hunter—is a typical anything. I think that's at least one sign that I've matured a little. Very little, some friends and family might say, but I've matured, nonetheless. If you replaced "crack" with "opioids" in the article, it would be an accurate representation of today's addiction climate. What would future Joel have been surprised to learn back in 1994? Perhaps most surprising is that Stallone is still making "Rambo" films! What else? The toddler being murdered in England still sticks with me today. At the time, it had a profound effect on me, likely because my own girls were toddlers at the time. Horror has no expiration date.

Aside from some side ventures into "how-to" territory, my writing has always circled back to a few themes. I started my authoring career with *Season of Obsession*, followed closely by *Thursday's Bird*. Those books embody the idea of cramming every last minute of enjoyment into every last day of hunting season. Lately, though, my books have been examinations of time. I didn't realize it until I re-read those books in preparation for this one, but it's true. I never set out to write about time, but that's what happened. Maybe it's just a natural extension of aging and the realization that time is not unlimited. *The Ghosts of Autumn* is about looking back at hunts and hunting partners past and celebrating those days. *Strong Is the Current* is about my daughter's death and the inescapable terror of not being able to make time stand still—to make the clock stop ticking to live just a moment longer in that elusive present. I suppose it's natural, then, that this latest outing should complete the unplanned trilogy of time and examine the future, such as it can be examined. Searching out the meaning in days that have not yet been is perhaps the most difficult pursuit of all.

I'm glad you're along for the hunt.

25

AGE & GRACE

A graceful and honorable old age is the childhood of immortality.
—Pindar

"THERE HE is," I said as we passed the red SUV in the pre-dawn darkness.

"You have to give him credit," Steve said.

I did. I gave him a *lot* of credit.

The hunter, plainly visible in the dark mere yards from the mountain road, wore a full blaze-orange outfit. His SUV was the same one parked in the same place where we had seen it going on five years. He always hunted very near the road, in the exact same place, camped out on a big, comfortable-looking folding chair. Once, two years ago, coming out of the woods slightly off course after trailing a deer, I walked into his line of sight and quickly veered away, hoping not to anger him by my intrusion. He couldn't have been nicer, telling me that he was

on his way out anyway, and asking what I had seen. He was a
fixture in that place. He wasn't there every time we hunted, but
he was there every year we hunted. On the day I was, well . . .
lost . . . it was the first we spoke. I guessed his age somewhere
in his late 70s. Not that *late 70s* is ancient, but it's a fair stretch
on in years to still actively deer hunt, and it went a good way
toward explaining why he always hunted near the road. Our
talk was brief, but he was old school. A nice, pleasant person
eager to share a word or two with a passing stranger on a lonely
hilltop. This was our first sighting of him this year. As usual, he
was in place long before daylight, and far earlier than us.

As we readied to make the steep climb to our respective hunting areas, eager to beat the sunrise, an orange figure approached
us on the road.

"Good morning! Which way are you headed?"

We told him.

"Okay, well, my brother is at the far end of the ravine and I
will be down in that stand of pines," he said, gesturing into the
darkness. We knew where he meant.

"Thanks for the heads-up."

It's always nice to run into nice people in lonely places, people who are concerned with making it a good, safe, and enjoyable hunt for everyone. Even a couple of strangers.

"And my dad . . . that's him down by the SUV. He'll be right
there," he said, adding a short laugh.

"We see him every year," I said.

"Yeah. He hasn't gotten out as much as he wanted this year,
but he wanted to come today. It's getting harder. He's 89."

89.

"God bless him."

I'm not a *God-bless-him* kind of guy, but that's all I could
think of. And I meant it.

"Yeah, he still loves to deer hunt."

"89."

"89."

In the growing daylight, I eyed up the son. He was older than me, maybe by as much as ten or fifteen years.

"That's just great," I said.

"He loves it, and he's still a hell of a hunter," he repeated.

We shook hands and exchanged wishes of *good luck* as polite hunters are known to do. The son seemed, much like his father, to be a decent man. It's good to run into gentlemen out in the wilds. It's not always the case. Selfishness doesn't exempt itself from the outdoor sports. I've seen it a bit too often, especially around something as passion-inducing as deer hunting and somewhere as potentially stress-inducing as public land. I wasn't the least bit surprised the nice old man had raised a nice younger man. Not surprised at all. Isn't that how it's supposed to work?

Once settled into the base of a large boulder, overlooking the same ravine I've overlooked many times before, I pondered the age issue. Writing this chapter from the distance of two months since that morning, I find myself pondering the sometimes harsh, involuntary act of aging even more than usual. Sitting at the old oak desk that used to belong to my great grandmother, my back hurts. I mean, it *really* hurts. In my fifty-second year, I've had arm pain, shoulder pain, elbow pain, numbness, tingling, you name it. And today? It's my back. I walked around my day job hunched over like, well . . . like and 89-year-old man. I discovered about ten years ago that I have two bulging discs. I elected not to have surgery and can usually remedy the pain by spending a few minutes for a couple of days on an inversion table, which Joy thoughtfully purchased for me several years ago. Today, though, the ten minutes on the table did nothing and I'm suffering. And no, this book isn't going to be an old man whining about his injuries. Well, maybe just this paragraph. But as I sit here typing, hoping the anti-inflammatories kick in soon, I ponder the realities of an 89-year-old man still feeling the pull to deer hunt. *God bless him*. 89. I do the math (with the aid of my calculator—I'm not a mathematician) and that's thirty-seven years older than me. The frame of reference I've been most reminded of this year is the difference between hunting when I was Porter's age (24) and how it feels now to be twice that old. I can't even imagine hauling myself out, even if it's just a few yards, into the woods from the car, to deer hunt with thirty-seven additional years under my belt. I feel pretty old right now. But, then, I guess I'm not *that* old. So, I'm telling myself, *suck it up, buttercup*. I probably wouldn't have thought at 24 I'd still love deer hunting just as much twenty-five-plus years later, but I do. I think age itself is a much more fluid notion as you get a little more of it. I constantly think of myself as younger than I am (I think that's the default, at least for men). But then, like today, my body reminds me that I'm not 24—like that frigid morning, crawling my way over frozen boulders on the shore of Lake Ontario with Porter and his friends. There are limitations that youngsters don't have accompanying the onset of middle and old age. It can be depressing, but it hasn't depressed me into not wanting to try yet.

I wonder what Porter and his friends, all about the same age in their middle-20s, think of me. Am I just an old guy to them? Am I (I hope) an *older* guy who loves to hunt? I don't know what's in their heads when I tag along. I'm not sure, but I keep getting invited to go hunting with them. Like the notion of age, perspective is also a hard one to nail down. Thinking hard about how Porter and company see me, I force myself to think of how I used to see my older hunting partners. There was John, about ten years older than me. I never really thought of him as older, but I did envy his additional years of experience and knowledge. It was the same for the old bunch of codgers who taught me to deer hunt. They were *much* older than me. But I didn't think about their ages. I thought of the wealth of knowledge they had, and I worked hard to absorb as much from them as I could during the short weeks of deer season. I hope that's how Porter sees me. It's possible that he has a completely different view than that. Whether it's ducks, deer, or fishing, at 24 he is a lot better at all of them than I was. He's getting his first hunting dog this year, a black Lab. I may be ahead of him in the dog-handling department, but it probably won't last.

I thought again about the old man, and my old man. My dad used to hunt with me. We did a lot of bird hunts together, and he even joined me for some Catskill Mountain deer hunts. I don't know that he enjoyed the deer hunting as much, but he was a good sport. He doesn't hunt anymore, preferring to spend his time chasing antiques. He thinks of it as his form of hunting. The old man by the side of the road is a testament to the hunter spirit. He's an inspiration and a fine example of aging gracefully, when old age itself can be cruel and, more often than not, graceless.

Being a grandfather myself for two years now, I wondered how many grandchildren his kids have blessed him with. More hope for the future of hunting, I pray. I turned the thoughts over and over in my head as quiet time in the woods often causes me to do. On the way out of the woods at noon, I hoped to see the old man at the edge of the woods, but he and his boys (*boys* who are older than me) were already gone. I wondered if I would see him again next year. If he can make the short walk from the car to the woods, I'm sure we will. He'll be 90.

My back feels better already.

26

A TALE OF TWO CELL PHONES

Our inventions are wont to be pretty toys, which distract
our attention from serious things. They are but improved
means to an unimproved end . . . We are in great haste
to construct a magnetic telegraph from Maine to Texas;
but Maine and Texas, it may be, have nothing important
to communicate.
—Henry David Thoreau

HANG ON, don't hang up.

Before you skip this chapter, thinking this is just an old-man-yelling-at-clouds type exercise and one that is best ignored, wait a second. It's not. I was the first among my friends and family to have a cell phone. I remember it well. It was a clunky Nokia that looked very much like a *real* phone receiver. That model—one of the first—was released in 1992. I got mine in spring of 1993. I liked it a lot, and still think that design was underrated. The first day I owned that phone, I traveled to the Oatka Creek for a fly-fishing trip to New York's Southern Tier to take advantage of a reported hatch of sulfurs. I love the sulfurs because (in order of importance), they're bright yellow, easy to see, and don't require any deft fly-tying skills to recreate them. From the parking area near the bridge, I could clearly see I was running a bit late and the sulfurs were already hatching. Judging by the dozens of rings and ripples on the surface of the calm, deep creek, it was time to get fishing. Only . . . I *didn't. Not yet.* Taking the shiny, new cell phone from my fishing bag, I called my friend, John.

"Hey, I'm at the Oatka and the sulfurs are hatching like mad! Oh, and I'm on a cell phone!"

John, an accomplished fisherman and a purveyor of plain words said, simply, "Why are you calling me and not fishing?"

Why, indeed? Because I *could.* And so began my long, tumultuous relationship with cell phones. By *long,* I mean twenty-eight years long. In those twenty-eight years, I have never been without one. And now, in 2021 I have two. One is for work, one is for home. As others have written about at length, our connectedness is both blessing and curse. My personal phone keeps me in touch with my family and friends. When bored out in the woods, I often read the news, or make notes for my next writing project. Every now and then, I'll take a photo, though I still prefer a real camera for most of those moments. Smartphones have indeed gotten very smart. The old Nokia is a fossil compared to the fun stuff now available on the sleek, newest phones.

That last day duck hunting on the pier, in between the decoying ducks, the boys were often glued to their phones, scanning only intermittently for incoming ducks. I had both of my phones on me, but they stayed in my coat. Not that I had a problem with using a phone during a duck hunt, but I genuinely didn't want to drop one of them onto the icy boulders and into the drink. While Porter and I watched for ducks, the three other guys stared at their phones. During that hunt, it dawned on me that most of them are in their mid-20s. Since cell phones have been around for the better part of thirty years, they had never known a world without them. To someone like me who still considers them *new technology,* that fact stood out like an old duck hunter.

I promised in this chapter's opening paragraph that I wasn't going to do the old man, get-off-my-lawn-with-your-damn-cell-phone routine. I'm not. I like being able to let Joy know I'm okay during a day-long deer hunt. I enjoy getting photos of my grandson while sitting in the quiet deer woods. I think cell phones are great tools. My GPS unit, once also considered high technology, has been rendered almost useless due to phone technology. Now, with the touch of an app icon, I can instantly get an aerial view of an area I'm hunting or thinking about hunting. Weather reports are similarly available, taking much of the surprise out of impending storms. Just using basic text features, I can send a photo or give an update to my hunting partners. I can even shoot a video of a passing buck and share it in real-time.

Is there a downside to all this connectivity? Sure. There are several. One is that you're *always connected.* Just as Phone Number One lets me communicate with my hunting partners, family, and friends, Phone Number Two ensures that I'm always available to take work calls. Though both phones are generally silenced, I must keep my work phone at least on vibrate, since I'm on call 24/7. When that phone vibrates, my heart jumps into my throat, and I reach for it with a sense of dread, wondering what's wrong. I'm so conditioned after years on call, that you might think I'd be used to it. I am not. Also, whether I'm deer or duck, pheasant or woodcock hunting, I pretty much *must* answer it. Talking about work issues while enjoying the quiet serenity of the hunt is an affront to everything I believe. That's just the way the world is now. Maybe Porter's generation, already slaves to their phones at a very young age, will never feel the stress-inducing nature of those calls. Maybe it will simply seem as natural as can be. I'm not complaining about it, mind you. Because of those smartphones, though, the world has changed. Is it better or worse? Neither, I suspect, but they have changed the way we live. The isolation of the lonely woods is still isolation, despite the text reminding me about next week's doctor's appointment vibrating deep in my coat pocket.

It's different.

My small circle of deer hunters has spread out. Only my brother-in-law remains geographically close. John has moved south. Porter is two hours away. In the past, when everyone was near, a nice buck being killed often resulted in a visit to the successful hunter's garage to see it hanging from the rafters. Very often, celebration ensued. Now, due to the distance, most celebrations are relegated to shared photos. Those photos aren't of deer hanging from garage rafters. More often than not, they're directly from the field while the deer is still warm. And that's okay. It's exciting. It's a window into the world of my friends and family that I might not otherwise have.

Deep in the New York deer woods, my personal phone vibrated. Eager to see if one of my hunting partners had scored, I checked the phone, swiping the screens with cold fingertips. It was John.

"Buck down!" The accompanying photo showed a handsome 7-pointer.

John was in Kentucky.

27

THE TIMEKEEPER

THOUGH MOST of my deer hunting this year was with Porter, I did manage to sneak in a few hunts with my brother-in-law, Steve. For the record, Steve is slightly *older* than me. There's no point in telling you that, other than to say that being the youngest guy on this hunt makes me feel a little better. Steve has hunted with me as long as I've been hunting. I'm pleased to also tell you that I took him on his first successful deer hunt many, many years ago. Since that early hunt, we've hunted together every year, both for pheasants and deer. In a side-by-side comparison, Steve and I are not a lot alike, at least on the surface. A second-generation German, he's fond of his routines and is an excellent planner. I am not fond of any routines and, though I'm capable of planning, I'm more of a drop-every-thing-and-go kind of person. I'm a springer spaniel and Steve . . . well . . . he's a German shepherd.

Arriving at this particular piece of state land, not for the first time, Steve commented, "We've hunted this place for sixteen total hours without either of us seeing a deer." I quickly did the math in my head. I should say, I *attempted* to do the math in my head. I know we hunted here a few times, each for a half day. I quickly gave up on the math, not because I couldn't do it, but more because I knew from years of experience that Steve was likely correct.

The last few years saw at least one deer come out of here each fall. One of the largest bucks I've ever seen on the hoof passed me in the very ravine we'd be hunting today. For the most part, however, this large tract of state land is one of the places that we'd go to fill doe tags, often successfully. But after four unsuccessful trips this year, it was less a venison run than it was a repeated exercise in frustration. We *knew* the deer were there. Their tracks, both old and fresh, trampled the hillsides. 2019 was just a strange deer season. After all the strange hunting seasons my merry band of hunters has endured, that is saying something.

Typically, we'd been hunting from the early morning to the early afternoon. This time, we planned to make a full day of it and not come out of the woods until dark. At the tailgate of the truck, we checked our packs to make sure we had phones, enough food and water to get through the day, GPS units, and all the other assorted goodies to make what could be a long day in the woods a little more tolerable. Wishing each other good luck, we went in our separate directions.

The temperature was frigid for the first few hours, but it kept me hopeful that might get the deer moving in daylight. Hunkered in at the base of a small boulder overlooking a sprawling, brush-choked ravine, I had a good feeling. I sat like a statue for a very long time. This was the first place I ever killed a deer here—a huge old cow doe when I was hunting with John—and I'd taken a couple since then in this very spot as well. Despite the poor track record this year, I had high hopes. I hadn't visited this exact spot since early last season, and figured it was time to see if some of the old luck might return. While my hands and feet grew uncomfortably cold for a half-hour or so, the sun soon shone down into the ravine, just in time, and warmed things back up to tolerable. By 11 a.m., I must admit I was surprised to have once again seen no sign of a deer. As with our last trip, fresh tracks littered the hillside, some passing within mere yards of my hideout. Through my binoculars, I could see the narrow funnel at the bottom of the ravine was also heavily tracked up. But . . . nothing.

Breaking my hands out of their wool gloves, I sent Steve a text.

"Seeing anything?"

"One squirrel."

Ouch.

At this point, the story is supposed to take a dramatic turn and, as the afternoon sun breaks out, a large herd of does will walk past me at fifty yards, offering me the chance to fill one or two of my doe tags. It really would have made a great story. Alas, the afternoon passed with nothing more exciting than a brief visit from a pileated woodpecker who jackhammered out his lonely staccato beat on a nearby dead beech tree. The few clouds in the sky disappeared as the sun set low in the deep, mature hardwoods lining the ravine. It started to get cold again. I checked the time and stayed ten minutes after legal shooting light, just to see if I could see a deer. I didn't. I took my time walking out of the snowy woods and down the hill to the truck. The snow and orange glow of twilight made walking in the darkness easy. Once at the truck, I noticed the orange from Steve's hunting clothes coming down the hill several hundred yards away. I must admit, there wasn't much of a spring in his step.

Once at the truck, I said "Well, that was a long day without seeing a single deer."

Steve simply said, "That's twenty-four hours without a deer."

He was, of course, right.

28

THE OVERVIEW

What is the good of experience if you do not reflect?
—Frederick the Great

LAST YEAR, late season.

It was still early for deer movement, and Porter and I talked quietly in a small opening in the brush, just below the field's edge. He pointed out areas where he had seen deer, coyotes, and eagles. Porter's enthusiasm for the natural world goes far beyond his natural gifts as a hunter and fisherman. His appreciation for all things wild puts him in a very small circle of hunting partners with whom I feel comfortable discussing anything.

An hour passed and what was left of a very slight north breeze dwindled into the dead, icy calm of a December sunset. Our conversation dropped off to a few hushed whispers, and then nothing. *Deer time.* We scanned the river bottom, surprised to see a doe in the brush only seventy-five yards below us. As so often happens in deer hunting, I had no idea where she came from. Farther out, toward the river, two deer emerged from thick brush and meandered in our direction. Even without checking them with the binoculars, I could tell by their short bodies and playful behavior, chasing each other in and out of the brush, they were fawns. Quickly turning my attention back to the doe below us, I whispered to Porter.

"She looks decent."

"Small, I think," was his reply.

She wasn't an old cow doe, by any stretch of the imagination, but I thought she was an adult deer, just by body shape alone. Though, after the season I'd had, I demurred to Porter's assessment, thinking to myself *I'm sure he's right.* I didn't want to shoot another small deer. Not even another *smallish* deer.

The doe disappeared before drifting back into our sight line, slightly farther out. She was moving steadily away from us, which was not at all part of the plan, as much as you can have a plan during deer season. When she turned broadside under a small apple tree, Porter whispered, "Maybe she's bigger than I thought." Still only one hundred and twenty yards out, I quickly traded the binoculars for my rifle and dialed the scope up. Now, it was my own assessment that she wasn't very big, though not extremely small. I felt my heart rate ticking up ever so slightly as I asked myself what I would do if I was alone. The honest answer is, being the last day of regular gun season, I would have shot her. I paused, trying to judge her again in the dying daylight. I put the gun down as the decision was taken out of my hands and she turned away from us, walking slowly back into the river bottom brush, tail flicking every now and again.

"She might have been bigger than I thought," Porter said.

"I think she might have been *smaller* than I thought."

We both laughed, no longer whispering in the last wisps of daylight.

In the darkening river bottom, we told more hunting stories

as the season wound to a close. Taking an overview of my intermittently bad season, as well as Porter's undeniably great season, we laughed again and again as we relayed the highs and lows of the year. The laughter was a burst of warmth in the chilly December air. Looking back on recent, as well as ancient, history is all part of the rich deer hunting experience. I wouldn't trade it for all the venison in the world. Not that I have much to trade this year.

As the sun sank below the far hills, we walked back out across the sprawling cornfield and toward the road. We had no way of knowing, of course, that in a few short days we would embark on a late-season muzzleloader hunt not far from here during which, in the space of a few short minutes, my deer hunting fortunes would turn on their ear.

That's a story for another day.

29

THE FUTURE

SEVERAL YEARS back, I sat in the office of a writer (the dreaded *outdoor writer,* and I considered him the outdoor writer to end all outdoor writers) with a successful and lengthy career in the deer hunting and wildlife photography business. As I pitched my book idea to him, he sat across his large, imposing desk from me, and fixed me with a steely gaze, his fingers locked into a steeple on the bridge of his nose. I was younger then and I'm quite certain now that my squirming was the source of some delight to him. When I'm nervous, I tend to talk more, and joke more. And, I'll be damned if he didn't make me nervous. I'd considered him an icon, and a hero to me both in his knowledge and his photographic skills. Once I wound down my shaky, ill-planned presentation of what I thought would make a nifty little hunting book, he leaned back in his chair and made me wait a bit. More squirming. More nervousness. When the silence finally broke, he said the project sounded okay. He didn't love it, but he thought we could probably sell it. I was hoping for a little less mercenary reply. I love to hunt. I love to write about hunting. I was disappointed that his only take on it was that it would *probably* sell. It wasn't my youthful inexperience. I write to share my passions and my experiences. If it sells? So much the better. He, on the other hand, had a different approach. I can't say that I liked it. We made an agreement for another meeting, when we'd iron out the details and talk to a publisher. I was eager to leave, my inner early warning system telling me this may not have been the best idea I'd ever had in my life.

Before I left for the long drive home, the outdoor writer to end all outdoor writers said something else. It was years ago, and I can only paraphrase, but what he said was that we should probably do the hunting book soon. I asked him why. He replied that he thought hunting, as we knew it, would likely come to an end in his lifetime. Essentially, he said that in a few years, no one would be hunting and a function of that is that no one was going to buy books about a sport that no longer existed. I was disappointed, dumbfounded, and it pained me to hear such negative words from someone so completely intertwined with the sport of deer hunting. To this day, I'm surprised at the level of negativity displayed that day. The writer, a generation older than me, passed a few years ago, and I was again reminded of his dire predictions for the future of hunting. As it turns out, hunting didn't end in his lifetime. As of this writing, it doesn't appear it's going to end in my lifetime (not if I have anything to say about it, anyway), but still, his death rekindled the memory and, in turn, begged the question: *What is the future of hunting?* A few days ago, I posed that exact question to a loose group of friends and acquaintances whose opinions I value. In some cases, the responses surprised me. In others, knowing the respondents and having spent some time in the field with them, they did not. I'll share them here with you. After these thoughtful responses, I'll give you my take on the situation.

My respondents ranged in age from 24 to 88 years old, and I've ordered them from youngest to oldest.

Zachary LaVenture (24)
I feel like the future of hunting is very hopeful as I see a large number of new young hunters adventuring out into the woods with their parental figures, learning the proper ethics of hunting. Personally, I've hunted my entire life, I'm 24 years old, and have been hunting with a gun in my hand since I was 12. My sister is 14 now, and just started hunting two years ago, and has already tagged two beautiful bucks. She told me that in her class there is a competition for the biggest buck of the year, and that 90 percent of her class participated in the competition.

Porter Hunt (24)
I think that unfortunately we are facing quite a bit of legislation that could change both conservation funding and how people hunt in the future. That could end up having a negative outcome. In general, at least from the number of younger hunters like myself that I know, it seems like there is definitely a future for all types of hunting. Lots of very motivated young people have the same drive and passion that you and I share. That's really what it takes, in my opinion. I could have a skewed interpretation of what the younger generation of hunters looks like just because those are the type of people I end up being friends with. I don't get along with 90 percent of my own generation (laughter). Most of my closest friends are much older or part of the select few young people that still have solid morals and interest in the outdoors.

Jeff Miller (37)
I feel like hunting has a bright future, especially "localvore" hunting. The sustainable use of our wildlife resources is at the

heart of hunting, and nothing is more natural than hunting and eating wild game.

Scott Rohe (48)

I feel the world of hunting that we grew up in doesn't exist anymore. So much has changed. What has stayed the same is the time spent in the woods. As the older generations quit hunting, it's important to teach the new generation how to put down the electronics and spend time in the outdoors. The kids are our future.

Dave St. Onge (51)

With the many distractions today for all of us, it takes real and focused effort to introduce someone new to hunting and fishing. But it's important . . . almost a duty, I feel, that we pass on what we've learned. After three years in the field (which really only amounted to a handful of days), my son took his first deer this past season. The look on his face was priceless! I'm not sure who was more excited, him or me! It's a day he won't soon forget, and one that I'll cherish forever.

Joy Spring (52)

I grew up in a hunting family and spent my childhood listening to the hunting stories of my father and uncles. I remember waking up and running to the window hoping to see a deer hanging in our maple tree. I never considered hunting myself . . . that was for the men. A few years ago, with Joel's encouragement, I took the hunter safety course. I was apprehensive going in, but to my surprise, the class was comprised of kids and women. I have been pheasant hunting ever since, and this year I saw several couples out in the fields together. I think the opportunity to spend time outside with my husband and my dogs, being able to appreciate and observe nature and wildlife, is priceless. I'm hopeful that more women will continue to be part of the future of hunting.

Arnie Jonathon (56)

The future of hunting in our nation has to be handed to our youth to preserve as a heritage. Without passing it down, it will disappear.

Bill Hilts, Jr. (60)

Hunting has changed from when I was a kid. Today's youth needs to connect with nature at an earlier age and we need to get them to put the electronics down. We need to expand our core base and encourage female and minority involvement. We also need to be cognizant of social media impacts, putting hunters and hunting on the world stage in a way that can serve as a public opinion influencer. I don't like the direction we seem to be headed.

Roger Page (65)

Even if I was on the fence about hunting's future, even if I held little faith in those asked to carry the torch, I wouldn't say so. I would not dare override my trust in knowing whatever our future depends upon will be there . . . and I turn to a formidable history as proof. So, yes, count me as optimistic.

Patrick Mahoney (68)

I think hunting has a strong future, but I believe politics tends to slow the growth. Certain states want to make it difficult to possess firearms and even more difficult for kids to have or use them. I think southern states will have better success taking kids out at age 10, some even as young as 8. New York, having to wait till 14, may be too late! By 14, most kids find something else to do with their time. I'm hoping with the life expectancy of people living longer, that grandparents may be the ones introducing kids to the sport. Seems that a lot of families need both parents working.

Chuck Branch (70)

A glaring observation after fifty years in the woods is the absence of youth. When I began with my grandfather in the 1960s, there were always teenagers tagging along and learning. How have we lost that following? How do we get it back?

Bill Hilts, Sr. (88)

Everything I read and see focuses on the problem of junior hunter recruitment. New York is the most restrictive state in the country when it comes to allowing big-game hunting with a firearm. That's certainly having an impact here. There doesn't seem to the interest in the junior clubs either, along with the mentors dedicated to educating them in the outdoors and the shooting sports.

Joel Spring (52)

Before I give you my take, I will just say that I'm delighted that my older respondents not only offered such deep, reflective thoughts, but that they also recognize that things need to change. Not content to watch our beloved sport slip away into an angry, uncompromising future where there is no longer room for hunting, they offer suggestions to preserve the sports with which we so deeply identify. For the younger respondents, my heart swells with pride at their replies.

I think there's a future for hunting. There was a trend toward divisiveness in the late 1980s and early 1990s that saw a hardcore anti-hunting movement take hold. When I discussed this with Porter not very long ago, he was surprised to hear me say that I think things are looking up. Perhaps it's due to hunters being better advocates for their sports or maybe it's that the general population realizes wildlife (especially deer) needs to be controlled in the absence of larger, non-human predator species. My own take on it is that people are very fearful of wolves and coyotes and, in their absence, are more willing to accept a human neighbor who helps to rid their areas of excess deer. The disconnect between anti-hunters, non-hunters, and hunters is a deep one. I'm of the firm belief that people who have not been raised in a hunting culture simply can't accept the idea that some of us *enjoy* the hunt. While little thought is paid to the folks who kill their chickens, fish, and cows, it's somehow less acceptable to share the landscape with a person who *enjoys hunting deer.* Having been a non-hunter early in life, I get it. There doesn't need to be a war. What there *does* need to be (as in so many facets of life) is a little bit of understanding. Hunters can't afford the mistaken image of hard-ass people wearing orange who blast everything in sight. Non-hunters can't afford to be people for whom anthropomorphism takes away their God-given common sense. Things are so polarized, socially, politically, and selfishly, that it's hard to find that common ground. Even sadder, that common ground has seemingly fallen out of vogue. To those of us out in the trenches, however, the common ground is where we must live. I don't judge non-hunters or anti-hunters. Taking a stand is another God-given right. I won't, however, sit back when someone with no experience with wildlife judges me.

We *can* all get along.

For hunting to survive, its advocates need to point out that all the early conservationists—Henry David Thoreau, Aldo Leopold, Teddy Roosevelt, and a long list of other examples—were all hunters. *Avid* hunters. Roger Tory Peterson, widely regarded as the original *birder,* also enjoyed the hunt. What needs to happen lies in educating the general public to the fact that the people who *pursue* wildlife, also most *revere* wildlife. There's no reason to think that can't happen.

Let's try to ensure that it does.

30

OLD SCHOOL

THE FLASHLIGHT beam bounced ahead of me, creating strange shapes and oblong shadows in the pre-dawn gloom. Backpack straps tugged and the rifle sling cut into my shoulder. It seemed like I had been walking for a long time. It always feels that way in the dark. Still, I felt positive and hopeful. Walking into the deer woods ahead of the sun always has that effect on me. Until something happens, anything can happen. Overhead the moon and Orion shone in the gathering twilight. It was a cold morning, perfect for deer hunting. The light dusting of snow on crisp leaves reflected the small strip of orange glowing and growing on the horizon. It could have been the lights from a distant city, but it wasn't. Not up here.

Part of my positive outlook was attributed to my destination. Several years ago, I discovered a small brushy draw in a gentle ravine. It was full of deer sign. In the flood zone of a brook feeding the main ravine stood the remnants of an ancient apple orchard. A few of the dark, twisted trees still bore enough fruit to interest the deer and their paths were cut deeply into the landscape. I'd seen decent bucks here the past few years, but fate had either already filled my buck tags, or worked it out so the bucks never presented a shot. It was a good place to hunt, but the deer hunting rules still applied, including the pesky little rule that things don't always work out. Things had worked out consistently enough on non-buck venison in the ancient orchard, though, that I was pulled for the fourth year toward this hidden gem. Through the darkness I went. The walk was worth the destination and, despite the area being a large and popular tract of public hunting land, I had rarely seen other hunters in this quiet area.

Crossing the last open goldenrod field before the ravine, I glanced up again at the growing daylight in the eastern sky. The stars were fading as the morning light increased. I hurried my pace toward the base of a large beech tree where I'd stake my claim and hunt the day away. Approaching the edge of the ravine, I scanned below for any telltale signs that someone else might be in the area. Just then, though, the unfortunate rule about things not working out kicked in once again. I found my flashlight beam met by another, shining directly in my face.

"Sorry. I'm hunting here," a young male voice said in the darkness behind the flashlight. He wasn't sitting by *my* beech tree, but close enough that I'd have to move on.

"Good luck," I offered cheerily in return to the unseen voice. I didn't *feel* cheery.

Part of public land hunting is having a backup plan for situations such as these. *Several* backup plans are an even better idea, but at least one *good* one is a must. Turning on the heels from my lucky ravine, I backtracked a few hundred yards and quickly dusted off Plan B. Heading northwest, I crossed the field in a different direction toward a distant creek bottom. I couldn't ignore the fact that twilight was beginning to transform into dawn. I checked my watch. Sunrise was in ten minutes and the

Plan B creek bottom was easily a twenty-minute walk. *Oh well.* There was no choice at this point.

I'd discovered the place in the creek bottom several years ago while trailing a buck through the freshly fallen snow, old school. Though I never caught up with the buck, his tracks led me through a saddle in a gently sloping creek bank. The saddle was subtle, but unmistakable as a regularly used deer crossing between the brushy bedding areas to the north and the open beech and oak hardwoods on the opposite bank. An ancient, oversized oak provided a natural blind perfectly overlooking the deer trail. The day after unsuccessfully trailing the buck, I staked out the trail at dawn and was rewarded with the sight of the biggest buck I've ever seen on public land. He crossed the creek, following three does just before daylight. He was quite far up the creek, not on the trail I had discovered, so I dialed my scope all the way up. Unfortunately, my window of opportunity was fleeting, and I was unable to pull the trigger on him. Walking directly away from me, he vanished into the timber.

With the vision of the huge, old buck so fresh in my mind, branded on my brain by the fire of frustration, I'm sure I muttered some ungentlemanly words. Just then, however, the buck appeared again, walking directly toward me, peeking around another large oak only twenty yards away. He came out of nowhere. Off balance, and facing the wrong way, I quickly spun around and raised the rifle. With the scope unfortunately still dialed up all the way, I saw nothing but a blur of brown in the crosshairs that might have been the buck—or a tree. *You amateur,* I chided myself. As I reached for the magnification dial on my scope, the buck vanished with a snort, putting every tree in the woods between us in several huge bounds. He looked like a horse running off in the distance, his rack larger than almost any other I had ever seen. I was heartbroken. To kill a buck like that is, for most of us, a once-in-a-lifetime event. To kill him on wide-open public land would have been my greatest accomplishment as a deer hunter.

But it wasn't.

On my GPS, as well as in my mind, I marked the location of his crossing as *Bad Luck Buck*. I thought *Heartbreak Ridge* was a little too over the top.

In the gathering daylight, I approached the *Bad Luck Buck* creek bottom crossing. Sticks snapped under my feet as I abandoned all manner of stealth. Well into the first ten minutes of legal daylight, I was behind schedule and I found myself hurrying. No longer in need of my flashlight, I searched for the large oak tree overlooking the crossing. If I'd taken a few deep breaths and scanned my surroundings a little more carefully, I'd easily have spotted the big tree, only fifty yards distant. I did not take any deep breaths, nor did I do *anything* carefully. I was exasperated, annoyed, and mildly panicked. Whatever focus I'd started out with at the truck this morning had completely evaporated into a feverish quest to quickly get set up for Plan B. Finally locating the tree, and realizing I was sweating far more than one should sweat on a frigid winter morning in the deer woods, I hiked in that direction, looking neither left nor right. I just wanted to get into place. Rounding the trunk of the old oak, I kicked the snow and leaves from the base of the tree and started slinging off my pack and my rifle. Whatever made me glance across the creek as I was hurriedly loading my rifle, I do not know.

Fifty yards across the ravine from me, a very respectable buck stood staring at me. I can only assume he'd watched me hike in, kick the base of the tree clean, and start to load my rifle. If I was going to inject a bit of anthropomorphism into his look, I'd say he looked like, *well . . . isn't this special.* He seemed utterly unconcerned until I quietly slid the bolt closed on my rifle. The buck departed at the click, trotting up and over the opposite ridge at what can best be described as a *leisurely* pace. I watched him through the scope (this time dialed correctly), hoping he'd pause for a look back and offer some kind of shot. Of course, he did nothing of the sort and offered only his big, flagging white tail. A moment after I spotted him, he was gone.

Bad Luck Buck strikes again.

It was my own fault. I've killed a lot of deer because I pride myself on *always hunting*. Whether hiking into or out of a spot, I am always looking, always hunting. This morning everything was thrown off. I panicked and subsequently blew what would have been an easy, fifty-yard offhand shot at a standing buck. Settling into the base of the tree, I could hardly believe it. Sometimes having bad luck like that feels like ice water poured down your back and, as much as I should have learned from my morning's lack of observation, I found it hard to concentrate. I did manage to focus on the buck's trail, hoping he might return. Two hours passed, however, and nothing happened. The buck hadn't been particularly spooked, but this was public land, where an adult buck is a much better educated animal than your average white tail deer. I scanned the tracks up the opposite bank with my binoculars and thought, *hmm . . . maybe he didn't go very far.* Convincing myself I could track the buck *old school* didn't take much effort. Familiar with the land beyond the opposite bank, I knew that several narrow ravines paralleled each other across the landscape running roughly north and south. It was possible the buck would crest one of those ridges, drop into a ravine, and stay put without putting on too much distance. At the very least, if I carefully crested each ridge, I might catch sight of him in the timber below.

What did I have to lose?

I gathered my pack, scraped up my confidence, and dropped into the creek bottom. Easily picking up the buck's fresh tracks among the snow-crusted oak leaves, I followed them as quietly as I could, constantly scanning ahead, waiting and watching before moving on. At the top of the hill, the track became more confusing. A main deer run ran the crest of the ridge before the next ravine, and his tracks mixed with the other, slightly older tracks. Instead of dropping into the next ravine, he followed the main deer trail down the ridge and into some thick cover. I slowed my pace, realizing that he could be hidden in the brush only a few yards away and it would be nearly impossible to spot him. His tracks once again broke off the main deer trail, meandering now into a soggy area full of brush and boulders and hidden springs. When the brush became too dense, I called off still-hunting. The buck would hear me coming long before I'd ever see him.

Game over.

Trying to figure a shorter route to the *Bad Luck Buck* crossing where I would hunt out the day, I stumbled across intersecting deer trails, most of them heavily used, in a dense stand of young timber. I followed each of the trails, with each of them meandering from different directions into the heavy brush. It was a perfect ambush spot just outside of a large bedding area. Looking for a suitable place from which to hunt, I selected an upturned pile of roots, slightly uphill from and overlooking the trail intersection. I knew this would be a great spot to catch deer returning to their beds in the early morning and marked the root pile on my GPS. I left the area quickly, hunting out the rest of the day at the *Bad Luck Buck* crossing without seeing so much as a squirrel.

This season, I returned to the public land with my brother-in-law, Steve, dropping him off at the *Bad Luck Buck* tree.

"Are you sure you don't want to hunt here?" Steve asked.

"No, I'm good."

You can have it.

I continued up the creek, following my GPS to the upturned roots. I moved carefully this time, cautiously. No hurrying and no stick snapping. Settling quietly in, I surveyed the trail crossings and the bedding area just to my south. For the first time in days, the sun shone in a blue sky and temperatures rose out of the 20s all the way up to a balmy 30°F. by early afternoon. My disposition was markedly better than it had been when last I visited this place.

In position only for an hour or so, movement in the brush to my right gave away a deer moving purposefully through the thick saplings. When it became apparent she wasn't going to come out of the brush into the larger, more open timber, I searched frantically out ahead of her for an opening. I found a six-inch hole between two trees and focused on it. When her shoulder passed into the tiny gap, the rifle roared, and the deer dropped in her tracks. It had been a trying season, and I was happy to have had even this small success.

The irony wasn't lost on me that the biggest buck I've ever seen led me to a place where I blew my chance at yet another buck, which led me to scouting the deep-woods bedding area that, the following year, gave me one of the smallest deer I've shot on that piece of public land. Still, dragging her out, I was content enough in the fact I had done it *old school.*

31

JUST ANOTHER NIGHT

SKINNING THE doe wasn't difficult. Skinning a *small* doe seldom is, and it's not as if this was the first small doe I ever arrowed. In the corner of the garage, comfortably seated on a small step-ladder, was my dad. He was presumably there to keep me company but didn't let an opportunity pass to tease me about the small, late-archery-season doe. I took it in stride. We'd spent many days bow hunting together and I know that, back in the day, Dad would have been just as happy to arrow a deer like this. He's of the philosophy that any bow kill is a good bow kill. It has been several years since he deer hunted with me, but once the ribbing was done, he repeated that philosophy once again. Immersed in the knife work, I'll admit I was happy to have the company.

Gun season was coming fast, but deer season was already in full swing, and there was a lot of work to be done. Even while Dad and I chatted, I found myself hurrying through the skinning. As I have one hundred times before, I cut off the lower legs, cut slits up the front legs and along the rear legs,

179

and began to pull. The skin came down easily. Pulling the hide down to the neck, I sawed the head off and set the whole head and hide aside. Pulling the big, blue cooler close to me, I began working on the backstraps. The long, parallel knife strokes came automatically. Once the straps were removed and in the cooler, I set about getting the front legs free. After all these years and all of those deer, I'm still amazed there isn't a bone attaching the powerful front legs to the deer. In a moment, they too rested in the cooler. Fishing around the hip bone with my long, old knife, I found the ball and socket and freed one of the rear legs. With my left hand, I guided it into the cooler as it fell. A moment later, the other hind leg was free and in the cooler. After hurriedly cutting out the tenderloins, I stripped the rest of the carcass bare.

Once the quarters were in the cooler and Dad felt he had done his duty keeping his youngest son company in the garage, he left. I couldn't take a break, however. Watching the clock, I hurriedly stripped down, washed the blood off of my hands and forearms, and changed into some cleaner clothes. Rapidly rummaging through the piles of hunting gear in my spare bedroom, attic, and garage, I assembled my deer hunting guns, some ammo, a rangefinder, a handful of paper targets, and, finally, hearing and eye protection. Three trips from the house to the truck and I was loaded for bear—or at least for deer.

The drive to John's house took about ten minutes. I had only a moment to reflect on the craziness of deer season. In two short days, the relaxing, stoic nature of archery season would go through its annual metamorphosis, changing into the exciting craziness that can be gun season. So much to do, so little time. But it's a good craziness and, as rushed as I felt, I also felt like a kid on Christmas Eve.

I met John, already setting the picnic table up as a shooting bench, in his backyard. With only an hour until dark, we quickly set up the targets. John let fly with several rounds from his shotgun, while I sighted in my revolver and my muzzle-loader. Those three guns have accounted for untold numbers of deer in the twenty years that we've hunted together, and neither of us was surprised to find that no scope adjustments were necessary. We shot until the very last minute of daylight—just because it was fun. By the time we were done with our final practice session of the year, we were both confident enough in our guns to know that any misses would our own fault, not our guns. Gun season was just two days away. John and I talked in the driveway afterward, standing at the tailgate of my truck. We talked about where we'd hunt opening day, what we were hoping to see, strategies and plans. We've had this conversation a million times before, and it was a good feeling to know that the excitement of the impending opening day was still as strong and as intoxicating as ever.

Back at home, Joy had just gotten home from work. We grabbed two tenderloins and half a backstrap from the cooler. Deer season dinner. There's no better venison than a freshly killed young deer. We didn't sit around long after the meal, though, as there was still much work to be done. The kitchen table on which we'd just eaten was quickly converted to a butcher's block. One by one, I fished the quarters out of the cooler and flopped them onto the large, wooden cutting board. Working as fast as I could, I freed the meat from the bones. Joy packed the steaks and straps and roasts while I cut and trimmed and sliced. Once the meat had all come out of the cooler, we quickly cleaned everything off and transformed the table once again, this time with my ancient meat grinder. The grinder is built like a tank and weighs almost as much. Each year I swear I'm going to build a rolling cart for it in the offseason, but by then the pulled muscles have healed and I've forgotten all about it.

Joy sliced up chunks of pork to mix with the venison, and the grinding phase of the operation was soon in full swing. We were wearing down as the evening was wearing on, having both put in long days at work even before the skinning, target shooting, and cutting had begun, but we pushed on. This is always hard work, but *good* work, and it always seems like we're accomplishing something worthwhile. Like canning jelly or making hot-pickled cauliflower, it's an old-fashioned, rewarding kind of work that is innately *fun* and, like those things, something that we can do as a couple. The fact that butchering your own deer is something so few people do anymore makes it seem that much more special.

Well into the evening, the old electric grinder wound down for the last time. The last packages of venison were stacked carefully in the freezer, leaving room in hopes that there might be another deer or two once gun season was under way. Joy and I worked together, tiredly cleaning up the mess and washing down the knives and cutting board and grinder parts. Once done, I was ready to head for bed. Then I remembered that the guns still had to be cleaned. I didn't mind. It's my favorite time of the year, and this was just another night at home during deer season.

This story was written from notes I took in November 2013, seven years ago. Filling in the details comes easily, because most nights during deer season aren't so much different. John has retired and moved to Florida. Our hunting time together, which used to be so ordinary, so taken for granted, is a rare commodity these days. But other than John's large absence, and the fact a bad back doesn't allow me to enjoy bow hunting much anymore, the nights during deer season still look a lot like that random night from my 2013 notes. The old grinder lives alternately in the garage and the basement. I still haven't built a cart for it, twenty-five years after it came into my possession (see: *bad back),* and it should probably be re-wired with a new power cord, but it's still going. It was an antique long before I owned it. I've often thought that if you dropped it from an airplane (assuming the plane could get off the ground), it could likely wipe out a small country. Joy still packages the venison as I butcher it on the kitchen table. We still eat fresh venison that same night. The air of excitement as opening day of gun season approaches has not waned one bit. Looking back seven years, or thirty years, I think the younger man I was would look at his future self and smile at the knowledge that the excitement is still alive and well. He might well smile in the fact that the traditions are, as well.

32

THERE COMES A POINT

I've got a great ambition to die of exhaustion
rather than boredom.
—Thomas Carlyle

SNOWFLAKES STREAKED in the stark beams of the headlight. For the fifth time, we pulled up to the small piece of state land that Steve and I would call home for the morning hours. Even before we glided to a stop, the truck rocked lightly from the pre-dawn wind. The headlight beams were dizzying as the snow intensified. This was not going to be a good day for deer hunting, but our track record here this season lead us to believe anything else was possible. This place, the center of which holds that sacred waypoint on my GPS known as *Bad Luck Buck,* where I blew it on not one but two bucks last year, was turning into *Bad Luck Woods.* Yet, here we were again. Last weekend's trip showed the area to be littered with deer sign and we had reason to believe that we would eventually *see* one of those deer that made all those tracks. With the wind and snow, however, I knew that this was not likely to be the day that broke the streak. Not likely at all. Just as I reached for the key to turn the truck off and get this hunt under way, movement in the headlights in front of us grabbed my attention. Something scurried across the road. It looked like a grouse, but it was at first hard to tell in the swirling, wind-driven snow. Only for a second, I got a better glimpse as she passed into the direct beam of light. I pointed her out to Steve.

"Hen pheasant," I said.

"Wow."

What she was doing out in the middle of a snowstorm is beyond me. Pheasants, even more than deer, usually seek out the thickest cover as refuge against an impending storm. High on a hill in deer country, seeing her was certainly unusual, especially when you factor in the weather. Strange. Maybe she just wasn't a smart pheasant. Come to think of it, maybe we were just not smart deer hunters. Between the bird and the two middle-aged hunters, none of the three of us were going to win any awards for intelligence that blustery, threatening morning. The truck rocked gently in the growing wind. No sliver of daylight appeared above the hills in the east today. The storm clouds were visible, though, in the barely growing daylight. Ominous, fast-moving gray clouds revealed themselves in between snow squalls. I leaned back in the seat and said, not for the first time this year, "I'm getting too old for this."

"Yeah. Wait till you're my age!"

I didn't want to get out of the truck. *There, I said it.* I wanted to just turn around and go home. Steve, older than me but much less of a morning person, would not have objected, I suspect, if we hadn't already invested an hour driving to the hills. The pheasant pecked around in the headlights for another moment or two before disappearing into some long grass to the south. I closed my eyes and could very easily have drifted off to sleep. It's not my style, but it is a style to which I could have easily adapted that morning. I knew the hunt would be uncomfortable and likely unsuccessful. Trying to harness some cosmic positivity, I thought maybe the hen was an encouraging sign. I tried to wrap my brain around and play with that idea for a few moments. All I could come up with was that Steve and I were as dumb as that bird. The bird, at least, had no choice but to be out in the weather. Okay, I guess maybe we were dumber than the pheasant.

As we had before, we stood by the tailgate, checking our packs and uncasing our guns. By the time we got moving, it was light enough to see without flashlights. The gray, threatening clouds raced overhead even more quickly as we started the long trek up the hill. No one else was there, although it was the third Saturday during deer season. Not even the old man who hunted near the road was anywhere to be found. I'm pretty sure that, at 89 years old, he was far too smart to try hunting on a day like this. Just us young, dumb 50-somethings.

Yes, sir, *the recklessness of youth.*

Steve and I parted ways. If we wished each other luck, it was lost on the wind. I wasn't worried that someone might be in my favorite haunt, high above the ravine. If seeing deer was highly unlikely, seeing another hunter way up here on a day like this was completely out of the question. Unfolding my comfortable chair, I tried placing it in the relative protection of a big boulder. It was snow-covered before I settled in. Checking that my scope covers remained closed during my hike, I loaded the rifle and placed it across my lap. To my left, my backpack quickly disappeared under a layer of snow. Shortly after, I did as well. I was nothing if not camouflaged. Having dressed for the expected weather, and still warm from the steep hike, I was quite comfortable as I settled into and became one with the winter wonderland. I suppose I was a bit *too* comfortable. I'm not one of those guys who falls asleep in the woods. Not *usually* anyway. I woke up and looked at my phone. A half-hour of daylight had passed, and I wondered grimly how many deer had walked by during my nap. If recent history was any indication, I consoled myself, that number would be exactly *zero*. I think the pheasant, Steve, and I were the only warm-blooded creatures silly enough to be out in this. Trees swayed and rocked. A gust of wind blew the snow off a small hemlock sapling next to me and right into my face. It was miserable. Had this been opening day, or even a few days into the season, my optimism would have carried me through the morning. Being on the downside of a long hunting season, my optimism dropped me on my head. I began regretting the trip.

There comes a point almost every hunting season when the exhaustion starts creeping in. My hunting season had started in mid-October and had not relented yet, here in early December. Depending on the year, I experience varying levels of burnout. With a week off in October spent hunting every day, and then the remainder of bird season seeing me hunt *almost* every day after work, I'm physically tired before deer season even begins. We typically do one last bird hunt on the Thursday or Friday before opening weekend of deer season. There's no resting in between. Our deer hunts vary in intensity, but this past year had seen a *lot* of walking to and from our hunting areas. I was starting to feel the exhaustion earlier. Only a few days into deer season, I found myself sleeping through the night. As an insomniac, sleep is one of the few positives to be found at that level of exhaustion. Of course, sleeping through the night still meant getting up at 3 a.m. for these road trips. Now, in the waning days of gun season, I didn't have much left in my tank. I was tired. I look so forward to bird and deer season, it's always mildly distressing to feel something like burnout, but it happens. And it happens almost every year, these days. As the snow piled up around me, I thought maybe I needed a few days off. They'd likely be days I regretted during the spring and summer when hunting season again seemed so far off, but I began to believe it was time to recharge my batteries and maybe do something crazy like sleep in until 5 a.m.

We didn't see any deer. You may have guessed that.

On the way home, while I navigated the increasingly treacherous roads, Steve asked, "Are you going to do any late-season rabbit or pheasant hunting?"

"Oh, probably. Ducks, too." *Why pretend?*

Steve nodded. He looked sleepy.

33

RECOVERY & RETRIEVAL

EARLIER IN the day, Porter and I spotted three does bedded in the two-hundred-acre cornfield. Beyond them, a decent buck was tending another doe. As we watched, hidden in the grass along the edge of the field, those two deer also bedded down. Five or six hundred yards away from them, we tried to figure out a way to put a move on them. The truth was, the field was too big, with too many escape routes to have even a prayer of pushing the deer toward one or the other of us. As much as I love a good two-person still-hunt, it simply wouldn't work in this situation. Porter glumly agreed. We both had doe tags to fill, but Porter still held a buck tag as well. Even through binoculars, it wasn't at all certain that this was the mature buck that Porter had held out for throughout the season. Knowing that my aching back could not handle a crawl out of the tiny depression in the field that *might* put us within range of the deer, I suggested that Porter might want to try it.

"What are you going to do?" he asked.

"I'll go sit in the 9-point stand and watch a parade of bucks I can't shoot go by and listen for you to shoot."

He laughed, but I wasn't joking. Porter hunts hard and all of the good luck it seems he possesses is the result of that hard work. If he is sporting a secret horseshoe under his hunting clothes, it's only because he put it there.

The parade of bucks turned out to be just a semi-enthusiastic battle between two fox squirrels. At one point, the larger of the pair climbed a tree next to my ladder stand and initiated a few aggressive barks in my direction.

"Don't even start," I threatened.

He left.

The afternoon, relatively warm compared to the previous nights' hunts, wound to a close with no deer sightings. With the last tendrils of legal daylight, I thought I heard a distant *pop*. And then another. *Porter?* Although he was a half-mile away, the shots sounded too distant to be him. When I was halfway out to the truck, the texts started coming. He had not one, but two deer down.

"Buck & doe."

I smiled. Porter's luck is not accidental.

I drove down the road to the big cornfield and met Porter in the darkness on a mud-slicked tractor path. He quickly and excitedly relayed the story. Successfully belly crawling several hundred yards to within three hundred yards of the buck and doe, he watched them, eventually concluding the buck was up to his standards. Porter is a very good shot and dropped him in his tracks. Knowing that he had gauged the distance correctly, he couldn't resist the urge to also take the doe when she turned broadside and presented a shot. She didn't drop in her tracks, rather running off the side of the field and dropping into the swampy creek bottom below. In his rush to ensure the doe was down, he circumvented the field, heading right to the place she disappeared. Locating her just as darkness fell, he realized he would now have to recover the buck in the gigantic cornfield in the dark.

We first tended to the doe. Lying in several inches of water in a spring-fed meadow, she had piled up at the base of a steep hill. I held the lights as Porter field-dressed her, inwardly groaning as I watched the doe's chestnut brown coat become saturated with water. Deer are hard to drag anyway. Wet deer are infinitely more difficult, and we had to drag this wet deer up a steep hill. Each taking a water-slickened leg, we pulled ourselves up the hill by grasping saplings with one hand and the deer with the other. It was a short distance, but it seemed like it took forever to get her back to Porter's truck. Oh, and the hill was dotted with multiflora rose, nearly invisible in the dark. We were both scratched up by the time we reached the truck, and the back of my right hand was bleeding profusely.

Ah, deer season, how I've missed you!

Porter had to rearrange the bed of his truck before we could swing the deer up in there. I wasn't in any hurry, breathing hard after the difficult drag. He had, you see, just picked up 1500 pounds of pig feed and his small truck was already quite full. Once that was accomplished, he said, "Let's go get the buck." If there was any impatience in his voice, I'm pretty sure it's only because there are any number of carnivorous creatures out there in the dark, more than happy to snack on his hard-earned deer. Driving out the sloppy tractor path, his truck bounced and groaned. I wanted to suggest getting off the mud and into the cut corn where he was less likely to bury his truck. Before the words formed, though, Porter veered off the path and into the cornfield, slightly increasing in speed. The springs in the back of his truck groaned as we crossed corn rows. This time the words made it out.

"Slow down or you're going to break your springs."

"This truck is tough."

Oh boy. More youthful confidence. That is not precisely what I was thinking, as I hung on for dear life.

Ahead of us, glowing eyes. I thought we'd located the buck. As Porter slowed, though, I realized that—much like we were— those glowing eyes were also bobbing up and down.

Coyote.

"I'm guessing we're close to your buck."

I'm pretty sure I heard Porter's teeth grit in the dark cab of the truck. We were, in fact, *very* close to the buck. So was the coyote. I have no doubt if we'd been five minutes later, that dog would have started eating the deer. Thankfully, as we exited the truck, the glowing eyes disappeared into the darkness. The buck was a good one. With a tremendous buck taken during bow season, this was perhaps a bit of a letdown for Porter, yet he still seemed pleased. As I'd watched him do with my buck on opening day, he carefully inspected his, looking over the rack, the body, the hooves and commenting the whole time on his findings. I appreciate Porter's appreciation for the animals he kills, and his curiosity as well. It's just another way of thoroughly savoring the moment, and the animals we pursue. Though we likely both wanted to get home to a hot shower, it was good to take that small slice of time and thanksgiving after a long day. It always is.

Porter had done well, taking two deer together at three hundred yards. I couldn't have done it, both in terms of the patience of the stalk and the execution of the shots, and I told him so. It was one hell of an accomplishment. In the glow of the flashlights, my nephew looked up at me and smiled.

I think he already knew.

34

INTENSITY

MY FRIEND John is fond of describing the act of deer hunting as *hours of boredom, punctuated by a few seconds of insanity*. It's paraphrased from another quote about war, attributed (probably inaccurately) to many authors, but it is as apt a description of deer hunting as any other I've heard. I love spending time in the deer woods. Though I certainly like to shoot deer now and then, I am rarely bored. There's always something to watch, always something to learn. And if it *does* happen to turn into one of those long periods of boredom? There's always news to read on the cell phone. This day was the antithesis of long hours of boredom. It jumped straight to the insanity.

Late in the deer gun season, Porter and I formulated a hasty plan to push deer down the brushy edge of a creek bottom. We both had doe tags to fill and, since we'd seen heavy deer activity along the edge, we thought it might be a good way to put some venison in the freezer. Porter would walk the narrow, brush-choked bank to me. Once he arrived at my location, he would go out in the open field and circle back around to the creek bottom a quarter mile away and I would push down to him.

It seemed like a good plan. In retrospect, it *was* a good plan.

Early in the morning, an hour before making the two-hour drive to the hunting location, I'd stood before my gun safe. I'm not a *gun guy*. I have some guns, and a few older ones for which I have a little reverence, but I don't lust after guns or own an ungodly number of them, as some of my friends do. To me, they are tools that allow me to practice the trade of hunting. I might have a couple more than I need, but I don't go crazy with them. My two main deer guns are a twenty-five-year-old Winchester bolt-action rifle, and a Taurus handgun that I've had going on fifteen years. I got the handgun bug after unexpectedly killing my biggest buck the first year I owned it. Since then, I've killed somewhere in the neighborhood of fifteen deer with it. As I got more and more deeply into bird hunting, and less and less into bow hunting, I found the challenge of getting a deer within close range to shoot it with a handgun an irresistible one. For many years, I hunted with little else. Gradually, I got better and better with the handgun and found myself taking longer and longer shots. Due to a change in locations that I hunted, and a few missed opportunities due to the limitations of the revolver, I eventually returned to hunting with my rifle. I couldn't begin to tell you how many deer I've shot with that gun. It has outlived most of my hunting clothes, several pairs of boots, and a half-dozen backpacks. Last season I had to put a new scope on it when, at a successful shot on a doe, the crosshairs disappeared, clanking into the tube of my long-time scope. I wasn't upset. Twenty-four years of life on a mid-level scope, with hundreds and hundreds of shots through it, is a pretty good record. I put the new scope on, and the gun never missed a beat. It always felt good in my hands and there haven't been many deer or bears that walked away once the trigger was pulled. Porter and I would be putting on close-quarters drives and the revolver would be ideal for the snap-shooting required. Still, at the same time, I hadn't practiced much with it recently other than to verify that the scope was still on. Also, there was the potential for longer shots in one of the expansive cornfields near the creek bottom. The .44 mag with its zero-power red dot isn't much use past one hundred yards. Porter's takedown of two deer at *three hundred* yards, not far from where we'd be hunting, added a little more weight to the decision. I puzzled a few more moments in the open door of the gun safe before grabbing the rifle and promising the handgun I'd take it out more next season.

Skirting wide into the cornfield, Porter cautiously approached the upper edge of the creek bottom and waved to signal me to get in position. Creeping as quietly down into the brush as possible, it was difficult to find a shooting lane. Finally settling on the upturned roots of a tree, I found a window of about two feet through which I could safely shoot if any deer ran past me. Porter (and hopefully a few deer) would be approaching from the right, and my only safe shot would be as they passed below me, broadside. The shot would be fifteen or twenty yards, depending on which trail (if any) they used. *Fast and intense* would be the order of the day. I suddenly wished I had the revolver. The big, outdated, red-dot scope produces a dot far too big for precision shooting at any distance but, still, is shockingly accurate at hitting where it's placed. I double checked my rifle scope and ensured it was dialed down to the lowest magnification. Any shot I had was going to be short and brushy. Not ideal for my rifle, but there was no sense worrying about it now.

If the push went well for Porter, it would only take him ten minutes to reach me at a slow walk. The cover was thick, but the distance was not great. I tried to sit very still, knowing full well deer may be on the move already. Almost ten minutes passed, and I began to hear twigs cracking to my right. Since deer—even deer on the run—are typically quieter than that, I assumed it was Porter. I assumed incorrectly. Through the thick screen of branches to my right, I spotted brown and white bobbing in my direction. Three does were on the move. Had their path not been blocked by a tree, they'd have ended up in my lap. The lead doe stopped momentarily, spotting me through the brush. I didn't raise the rifle, figuring Porter must be right behind them. The three cut suddenly downhill before pausing behind a large, gnarly thorn-apple tree. The smallest of the three was in plain sight, fifteen yards from me. The two larger does paused perfectly so the tree obstructed my shot, because that's what they do. Using the cover of the tree trunk to hide my motion, I raised the rifle and put the crosshairs on the shooting lane, just three feet from where the trio stopped. If one of the two large deer took another step or two, there would be some more venison in the freezer, I thought. When you haven't yet shot a deer, I highly discourage having these kinds of thoughts. It's like seeing a big buck on the hoof and wondering where you'd hang it on the wall. That kind of thinking is simply ill-advised.

I do it all the time.

The three deer suddenly bolted. Two of them went straight downhill, keeping the tree between us while the third—the largest doe—briefly appeared in my scope as she passed through the narrow shooting lane. Had I been carrying my .44, she would have been more than hypothetical venison. I was carrying my rifle, however, and, even on low magnification, she was just a brief brown blur. I could have hit her, but the shot would have been irresponsible. After passing through my small window of opportunity, she raced downhill to join her traveling companions. Three white tails flagged off into the swampy creek bottom.

It all happened in less than thirty seconds. I must have been holding my breath. It suddenly came out in a raspy exhale, forming a cloud of condensation in the cold air. When Porter arrived, covered in burrs, he let me know that he'd never seen or heard them. I wasn't surprised. The cover was plenty thick to hide their escape. Perspective is a funny thing. To Porter, that brief little hunt was an aggravating, burr-covered walk in the woods without seeing any deer. On my end, it was one of the most intense hunts in many weeks of deer hunting, having three deer at point-blank range and not being able to do anything about it. As Porter started picking the huge clumps of burrs off his coat, I wondered if he noticed that my hands were shaking.

If he did, he was polite about it.

35

SOME ADVICE FOR YOUNG OUTDOORSPEOPLE

If we did all the things we are capable of, we would literally astound ourselves.
—Thomas Edison

IF YOU can't get the young hunters in your life to sit down and read for more than a few moments, bookmark this chapter, and be sure to say *it's short* before handing them the book. It's not an old man yelling at the sky. It's a later-middleaged man desperately hoping to pass on some wisdom in a world where wisdom is not valued as it once was. There are only two short pieces of advice, but I think they're worth contemplating.

#1. Life is short.

When you're young, you cannot grasp this concept. Know this. A million writers from a million different genres have tried to send this message, with varying degrees of success. I didn't start to become aware of the shortness of life until I was in my mid-30s. During the fifteen or so ensuing years since I started learning, I've learned a lot more. When my daughter Jennifer died at 23, the lesson was what should have been the early dawn of her life was not. It was the very end. Her entire life consisted of those twenty-three years. I'm proud to say she lived it well. One of the most frustrating parts of my life has been watching friends and loved ones say, *I can't wait to retire.* Even more insidiously, I hear their dreams of writing a book or opening a business discussed as if those are some far-flung goals to save for a rainy day. I think a huge number of people (perhaps, sadly, the majority of them) *don't* realize that every day, every hour, every minute and every second, life is not just *passing* by, but it is *racing* by. Be aware of the shortness of life, and you will begin to unlock the secret to a good life.

   #2. Live your life fully.

Tied inextricably to the shortness of life is the fullness of life. If I die tomorrow, I feel as if I've lived a full life. I've had adventures, made treasured friends, loved my family, and spent a good many hours trying to help others enjoy those moments. Still, there's more I want to do. There are more new things I want to try. I recently joined a Facebook group about kayak duck hunting. How fun does that sound? It has me more looking toward autumn than anything in recent memory. How will I fit it in between deer hunting and pheasant hunting? I don't know! I will, however, make it work. This is the second lesson I want to pass on. While lifetimes can be short, you have more time than you think. You can do more with that time than you believe you can. If you spend any great amount of time wallowing in boredom, you are doing life wrong. In the *Future* chapter, a couple of my respondents said we need to get the next generation to put their electronic devices down. At the risk of sounding like an old rebel, I disagree. I would only suggest engaging in activities as often as you can that make it worth sending a photo to your friends. Live! Be adventurous! In the huge, wide world of outdoor opportunities that exist for hunters, fishermen, and photographers, there are no good excuses for boredom. Get out there! Have fun! It's simple advice but, as you take a look at those around you, you'll see a lot of lonely, self-absorbed, depressed people. Don't be one of them. Better yet, if you can, drag some of those people out into the woods and share your passions with them.

That is all. Lesson over. Now go do something.

36

END OF THE HUNT

The beginnings and endings of all human
undertakings are untidy.
—John Galsworthy

IN THE glare of my truck's headlights, Porter's truck undulated back and forth in front of me. His own headlights blinded me as his truck struggled to find a grip on the icy, greasy tractor path, sliding from side to side, attached to my truck by a bright yellow tow strap. My truck, buried in several inches of ice, floating on a sea of mud, did not budge. While deer season began an unexpected comedy of errors, I never suspected it would conclude in the same manner.

I wanted to end the season by switching up locations, taking up a new post several hundred yards from the location where I shot the big buck on opening day. Parking my truck at a familiar corner of the big grain field, I tried to be proactive, making a U-turn so it would be pointing in the right direction up the tractor path when I returned to it after dark. That was my first mistake. It turned out to be more of an L-turn. The rear tires of my truck spun helplessly on the ice. I got out and surveyed the situation. Having experienced these things a time or ten, I didn't panic. I got back in the truck and put it in low gear, hoping to creep my way off the ice and back onto the tractor path. When the back wheels suddenly broke through the ice, the rear end of the truck dropped four or five inches, and I may then have panicked. I got out again and checked the situation. With my two-wheel-drive truck, there was no hope of getting out of this mess without help. With only a few hours to hunt before dark, I unloaded my gear, dressed for the cold afternoon. Hustling down the tractor path, carrying my pack, chair, and gun, I tried not to slip on the ice. I'd gone three-quarters of the way to the funnel area I wanted to hunt when some drifted snow revealed a double set of boot tracks headed in the same direction. I didn't have to be an expert tracker to realize those tracks, an adult and a child, were fresh. When they branched off toward the same trail I wanted to hunt, my exasperation doubled. While the altruistic side of me was glad that someone had taken their kid out deer hunting, the other side of me . . . well . . . he can be a jerk.

Hoofing it back up the slick trail, I passed my stuck truck and quietly groaned. Maybe it was my imagination, but it looked like it had sunk farther into the icy muck. I tried to ignore it, quickly formulating a backup plan so I wouldn't lose any more time. Each of the bucks I'd seen from my opening day stand had come from a small funnel between the big cornfield and a small thicket. A few dozen stately oaks lined a nearly hidden deer trail. All season long, I thought about hunting that place. With time at a premium, I looked around at the cover and quickly selected a spot that would allow a shot out toward the corn in one direction, and a clear shot up into the woods in the other. Nestling in the top of an old, fallen beech, I tried to calm down. My nerves aren't usually fried going *into* a hunt.

The two hours I had remaining to hunt, though the last deer hunt of the year, found me twitchy, cold, and unable to get my mind off my truck. The ever-present fat fox squirrels raced around the branches of the beech tree, twice passing within arms' reach. Normally, that would have amused me. It didn't. I decided to send Porter a text.

"Do you have a tow strap? I buried my truck."

"Yes. I'm watching a nice buck and some does. Don't worry, I'll tow you after dark."

Who, me? Worry? Needless to say, I spent the remainder of daylight worrying. It's no fun when your escape from worry becomes worrisome. I don't mind a little excitement in my deer hunts, but I'd prefer it be of a different kind. The afternoon passed without a deer sighting. Even the squirrels disappeared, leaving me alone with my worries. Back at the truck after dark, I loaded my gear into the back but kept my heavy hunting clothes on, not at all confident we'd be pulling the truck out. The bright moon shone down, illuminating the field. Three deer stepped out into the grain field, their dark shapes only fifty yards from my truck. Porter's headlights bounced up the slick tractor path and he skidded to a stop right at my front bumper. Walking around the truck, he said, "Oh, we'll get it out," as if reading my mind.

The confidence of youth. I miss that.

His truck spun and spun. It swerved unnervingly from side to side. After five minutes of unhealthy strain on his truck's transmission, Porter climbed out and again surveyed the scene.

"I may have to gun it to pop you out of there."

Once back in the truck, I braced for impact as Porter nosed his truck all the way up to my truck's grill. He reversed, stomping the gas. As the slack in the tow strap came to an end, I put the pedal down as well. The rear of the truck levitated out of the muck and ice. I hand-signaled Porter to keep going a few more feet, to be sure I was clear of the trap. I was. I thanked him as I knelt in the icy mud to remove the strap.

"Fun, fun," I added.

"It's always something."

The moon shone brighter now, and I pointed out where the three deer had materialized in the field. They had long since disappeared in all the commotion, of course. Back in the woods, two great horned owls hooted into the cold night. It would be a few weeks before I'd look upon that last hunt with any semblance of fondness, but I'm there now. It was a bad night, but it was also one more adventure to remember in a long line of adventures with a long line of hunting partners. I thanked Porter again.

"It was a good season," I said.

"A very good season!" he said enthusiastically.

Even against the afternoon's aggravation and nightfall's bitter cold, my renewed hope for the future warmed something deep down in my heart.

37

WINTER SOLSTICE

DECEMBER TWENTY-FIRST. The shortest day of the year.

The winter solstice is upon us. For me, deer season ended four days ago. There will still be some small game hunts, maybe a few duck hunts but, for me, hunting season has wound down and the long western New York winter is staring me in the face. I'm tired. It will take a week or two to recover. Maybe more. I put everything I had into bird season and deer season 2019 and the tiredness is pervasive. Nagging numbness in my left hand, pain in my left shoulder and my right elbow will only now get a reprieve from carrying heavy guns and gear, day after day, for weeks on end. Aside from physical tiredness, the mental tiredness is equally as real. As much as I love hunting, the energy required to maintain that level of focus and enthusiasm leaves me drained by the end of December. I would like to say it's always been this way but, no, it hasn't. Age's cruelest stroke is the dwindling of that youthful energy. I try to think of the old man on the hill and, at 89, how he must feel by December twenty-first.

The guns, so lovingly tended to on June twenty-first, in anticipation of this season now past, were disassembled, cleaned, put back together, and carefully placed into the safe four days ago. Still, the carnage of a full autumn of hunting is everywhere. Mini piles of hunting paraphernalia exist in the garage, the living room, the basement, and especially the back bedroom. It always proves to be a dumping ground, since it's out of sight of any visitors we might get. Layers of bird hunting clothes and gear lie buried under piles of deer hunting clothes and gear. It's a mess. The garage is even worse, but first things first.

Several years ago, when I was unable to locate multiple items that belong in my backpack just before hunting season, I made a pact with myself: At the end of each December, I would do my best to re-organize everything before retiring for the winter. Though I was tired, I wanted to uphold what has so far been a successful resolution. I started tossing things into slightly more identifiable piles. From those piles, I extracted items belonging in the hunting boxes I carry in my truck during the season, the hunting clothes racks in the basement, and several storage bins. One item at a time, I placed each item where it belonged, requiring many trips around the house and up and down the cellar stairs. In fifteen minutes, the back bedroom began looking once again more like a back bedroom and less like the Bargain Cave at Cabela's. Once completed, I moved out to the garage, where the piles were even higher than the ones in the bedroom had been. With a heavy sigh, I repeated the process. While pre-season planning is fun, there's nothing exciting about post-season cleanup.

Last things last, I emptied the backpack. Empty sandwich bags that held venison jerky and even the occasional sandwich were tossed into the garbage. I took the remaining items out. Knives, flashlight, pens, tags, first-aid kit, ropes, extra gloves, socks, and hats made yet another sub-pile. Stepping outside the garage, I gave the old camo backpack a vigorous shake and a surprising number of leaves and sticks fell to the ground. You'd have thought I'd been dragging the backpack behind me on the ground, rather than carrying it on my back. Maybe it had been two seasons since I last emptied it? It's possible. I have *tried* to be organized, with only varying levels of success, truth be told. Once clean, or clean *enough* anyway, I repacked the pack, remembering to remove the batteries from the flashlight and the GPS unit before their long, winter nap. Closing the zipper on the pack, I stashed it in a storage bin in the basement. A few years ago, I stored it in the garage which worked fine until the following autumn, when I had to evict the mouse living in it. He wasn't happy (neither was I—I may even have shrieked) and I wanted to avoid any similar drama next year. The bin's lid snapped shut with a definitive click, signaling the end of Hunting Season.

Returning to the back bedroom, I double checked that the gun safes were secure, casting one more glance at the bird and deer guns before retiring them for the winter. Outside, a dusting of fresh winter snow painted the frozen ground white, the condensation on the window lending a surrealist quality to the view. Later, sitting on the couch with a fresh cup of coffee, it felt good to put my feet up for a few minutes while it was still light outside. Max and Fred took up the opposite end of the couch, sleeping peacefully. It would only be a few days before I would start to feel the pull of the hunt again. First for ducks, and later the occasional rabbit hunt. For now, though, I was content. Having been through this for a decade or three, I knew it wouldn't last long.

38

THE CIRCLE

*Friends and acquaintances are the surest
passport to fortune.*
—*Arthur Schopenhauer*

THE TEXT came through just before dark. It was not a new occurrence. Over the last many years, I've gotten texts with lots of first deer and first ducks, first pheasants and first bear. This one, though, was a little more special. I'd been there for Melody's first pheasant and was hoping to be there for her first deer as well, but it wasn't to be.

"Mel got a doe. One-hundred-and-fifty-yard heart shot!"

I sat back in my office chair for a moment, looking at the dark, grainy cell-phone photo of Mel with her first deer. My own smile was equal to or greater than hers.

"I think I'm even more excited than her!" Porter continued.

I may be more excited than both of you.

Several puzzle pieces clicked firmly into place as I gazed

at the pictures and the accompanying text. Mel had her first deer. A new convert into the hunting lifestyle is a good thing on so many levels. Who knows how many people down the line *she* will affect or, perhaps, *infect.* Many, I hope. My day spent alone with Mel in the pheasant fields taught me that she'd come from a hunting family but didn't have a lot of interest in it when she was younger. She had, however, been a victim of Porter's boundless enthusiasm for hunting. I've been hunting a long time, and Porter's enthusiasm has no less an effect on me. However it happened, we need more Mels in the hunting ranks.

Perhaps more important than Melody's success, I found myself exceptionally proud of my nephew. That he was more excited than Mel said a lot. Becoming a hunter involves many phases, many steps, and many changes in perspective. Porter is hitting the phase very early in his hunting career in which he is starting to feel the strong desire to share, teach, and guide. It took me far longer to get to that. Porter is ten years ahead of where I was at his age. The pride in his texts about someone *else's* deer told me all I needed to know. I've watched Porter with his circle of similar-aged friends, and he is a natural-born leader. He's also a good example of what it takes to be a great hunter. I've learned a lot from him, though I probably wouldn't admit that to Porter.

Years ago, I had a favorite fishing writer in Paul Quinnett. He's still my favorite fishing writer, now that you ask. I hate to saddle him with *fishing writer,* since he is an accomplished author in many regards, particularly in the field of suicide prevention. Well, at least I didn't just call him an *outdoor writer.* After finishing his excellent book, *Pavlov's Trout, I* wrote Mr. Quinnett a letter and attached a copy of *Sports Afield* in which my first fishing article appeared. It was sometime around 1992. In my letter I mentioned to him how his writing had been an inspiration to me, and that my inspiration for the story in the magazine could be directly traced back to a chapter in his book. Only a week or so passed when an envelope with a return letter from Paul Quinnett arrived. Of the many kind words he wrote, the line that has stuck with me for the past twenty-eight years is this: "Is this how the circle continues? I believe that it is." I still have that letter somewhere. It had a profound effect on me that continues to this day. One of the things it taught me was, it takes very little effort to reach out and cross the void between strangers. It only takes a little effort and just a few words of encouragement to spark a fire that may last a lifetime. After reading Mr. Quinnett's letter, it lit a fire under me that provided the most productive phase of my entire writing career. To this day, I answer anyone who reaches out to me. It's the right thing to do. I read back over Porter's excited texts once more, looking again at Mel's beaming smile. Is this how the circle continues?

I believe that it is.

ABOUT THE AUTHOR

JOEL SPRING is the author of six books, including *The Ghosts of Autumn, Strong is the Current,* and *The Ultimate Guide to Kayak Fishing.* In addition, Joel has written an e-book about wildlife photography titled *Lessons from the Owl Tree.* He is a frequent contributor to *Deer & Deer Hunting* magazine. Joel makes his home in the small town of Ransomville, New York, with his wife, Joy.